D1553966

Storythinking

NO LIMITS

Edited by Costica Bradatan

The most important questions in life haunt us with a sense of boundlessness: there is no one right way to think about them or an exclusive place to look for answers. Philosophers and prophets, poets and scholars, scientists and artists—all are right in their quest for clarity and meaning. We care about these issues not simply in themselves but for ourselves—for us. To make sense of them is to understand who we are better. No Limits brings together creative thinkers who delight in the pleasure of intellectual hunting, wherever the hunt may take them and whatever critical boundaries they have to trample as they go. And in so doing they prove that such searching is not just rewarding but also transformative. There are no limits to knowledge and self-knowledge—just as there are none to self-fashioning.

Storythinking

Angus Fletcher

**THE NEW SCIENCE OF
NARRATIVE INTELLIGENCE**

Columbia University Press
New York

Columbia University Press
Publishers Since 1893
New York   Chichester, West Sussex
cup.columbia.edu
Copyright © 2023 Columbia University Press
All rights reserved

Cataloging-in-Publication Data is available from the
Library of Congress.

ISBN 978-0-231-20692-1 (hardback)
ISBN 978-0-231-20693-8 (trade paperback)
ISBN 978-0-231-55672-9 (ebook)

LCCN 2022050211

Columbia University Press books are printed
on permanent and durable acid-free paper.

Printed in the United States of America

Cover design: Chang Jae Lee

For Marlowe
inventor of the moon balloon

Ruminate strange plots.

—SHAKESPEARE

Contents

1

Story

Story.

It's for communicating ideas, not producing them. Sure, story is capable of inventing fantastical notions, but that's not real intelligence. Real intelligence is thinking critically, pushing past plausible anecdotes and beguiling fairy tales for true facts and enduring principles.

That's what I was taught in school. Which is why I was also taught that story's active form was *storytelling*.

Storytelling is writing or speaking a narrative, like when screenwriters type out movie scripts or when physicists explain the Big Bang in cartoon strips. Which is to say, it's fiction or rhetoric.

Fiction, my teachers warned me, was dangerous. Because really, "fiction" was another word for lie. And rhetoric was worse. It was lies that tried to seem legitimate.

Yet then came a surprise twist: fiction and rhetoric could also, my teachers revealed, be true instructors. A comic book could inspire kindness. A persuasive essay could share knowledge.

How was this possible? How could lies advance the truth? And why? What caused our brains to learn from fables? Was it a mental quirk—or something deeper?

I was mystified—and hooked. I'd long been entranced by the power of stories: *The Lord of the Rings, Frankenstein, Othello*. Making me wonder: Had my favorite books taught me right, or wrong?

And beneath this question lay an even more intriguing one: What was the secret to truthful storytelling? Find that secret, and classrooms could be filled with enchanting textbooks, rescuing students from boredom and confusion. Find that secret, and propaganda could be dismantled, ending the reigns of brainwashers and demagogues.

2

Excited by the prospect, I set out on a hunt for answers. After training for four years in the late 1990s in a Michigan neurophysiology laboratory (puzzling over how brain cells spoke to one another), I did a PhD in literature at Yale (puzzling over how Shakespeare spoke to me), then went west to Stanford for a postdoc, where in 2005 I encountered the field of narrative theory.

Narrative theory deployed a mix of literary tools (some more than 2,300 years old) to dissect novelistic plots and cinematic characters. Fascinated by the resulting insights and wanting to glimpse further, I paired narrative theory with a few neuroscience techniques I'd learned at the Michigan lab. The most spectacular were gadgets for peering into skulls; the most significant was a biology-based method: while previous researchers had scoured the stories of paper libraries and digital archives, I focused instead on living authors and audiences, trying to catch narrative's action in the way that a naturalist would net wild butterflies. I spent years in Hollywood and in MFA classrooms, attempting to pinpoint the elusive physical moment when stories sprang to life. I subjected thousands of book readers and theatergoers to weird experiments designed to capture the alchemical second where narrative fused with human consciousness, transforming it.

And as I did all this, I made an unexpected discovery: my teachers had taught me story wrong. Story wasn't just for telling. It was for something far more fundamental.

Story was for thinking.

STORYTHINKING

Storythinking hails from a time prior to authors, prior to humans, prior to language. It dates back hundreds of millions of years to the first creaky machinery of the animal brain. And its initial springs can be traced before even that, all the way to the earliest days of evolution by natural selection. Which is to say: all the way to the origins of life.

The origins of life were: creative action. Or in scientific lingo: reproducible new functions. That innovative conduct enabled the earth's first species to adapt to the Precambrian sea. And it also enabled those species to out-adapt each other, winning every changing instant of the tide's dynamic web of traps and assets.

More than a billion years ago, creative action became the function of whip-tailed prokaryotes, and a little more than 500 million years ago, it became the function of neurons. Neurons were, in their initial incarnation, insentient, so they didn't mean to act creatively. But just as natural selection had innovated unintentionally, so did neurons develop a mechanical procedure for cranking out fresh

3

biological activity. The method was to flail experimentally and adjust to feedback, trial-and-erroring into beneficial new movings and makings. From these primeval beginnings, creative action became the function of the vertebrate nervous system, which (sometimes consciously and other times impulsively, improvisationally, spontaneously) linked together neurons into novel sequences of hunting, dodging, building, singing, loving. Until finally, a few hundred thousand years ago, creative action became a function of the human brain.

The human brain empowered our Stone Age ancestors to respond to unpredicted challenges and opportunities by linking creative actions into new plans—which is to say, new plots. That hatching of plots was narrative cognition. Aka, storythinking.

Storythinking is contemplating *why* and *what if*. It's conjecturing from causes to effects. It's envisioning the consequences of different rules for action. It's mentally modeling hypotheticals, possibles, counterfactuals, and other kinds of *could happen*. It's using our cerebral machinery to stick original characters into never-before storyworlds and speculate on what happens next. It's natural selection, imaginatively accelerated.

Thus it was that storythinking became a tool of human intelligence. It refined the cruelly inefficient mechanics of Darwinian evolution into a motor of purposeful growth, helping us plan better futures and the individual steps to bring those futures to be. With storythinking, our forerunners dreamed up the republics, renaissances, and rocket ships of our today. And with storythinking, we continue on the narrative, inventing political revolutions, artistic movements, and technological contraptions—then plotting out the actions to hammer fantasy and sci-fi into tomorrow's fresh realities.

How had my teachers not seen this? How had they reduced story to communication? How had they not recognized that it could be a mental engine of practical problem solving and real-world innovation?

The answer is: my teachers had listened to the philosophers. And the philosophers had convinced my teachers— and just about everybody else—that intelligence sprang not from story but from logic.

THE LOGIC OF THE PHILOSOPHERS

The philosophers materialized more than five thousand years ago, all across the globe. They appeared in Sumerian Mesopotamia, Fifth Dynasty Egypt, Bronze Age India, the archaic Mediterranean, Spring and Autumn China, Classical Mesoamerica, and no doubt many other ancient sites whose history has quicksilvered from our annals.

From the beginning, the philosophers argued relentlessly. They disputed over where the world came from, what it was made of, and why we humans were here. Yet they could nevertheless concur on one thing: story wasn't a reliable tool for thinking. It was too idiosyncratic, too arbitrary, too fact-independent. So, the philosophers devoted themselves to finding a more rigorous thought instrument. And gradually they came to agree: that instrument was logic.

Logic's workings were discovered in bits and pieces by a disparate host of independent reasoners, ranging from the semimythical Saptarishi of the Hindu Vedas to the semihistorical Seven Sages of preclassical Greece. Until in 350 BCE, the scattered suppositions of those musing intellects were regularized, integrated, and unified by the Macedonian polymath Aristotle in the *Organon*.

The *Organon* consists of six books that lay out the formal rules of induction, deduction, interpretation, and dialectic. Those rules became the foundation of philosophy in much of the Roman Empire, West and East; then in most of Golden Age Islam; and finally, from the twelfth to the sixteenth century, in every great Western university, from Bologna to Paris to Oxford.

This reign of logic was challenged during the European Renaissance, when empirically minded natural philosophers such as Leonardo da Vinci, Galileo Galilei, and William Harvey abandoned (and even attacked) their Aristotelian schoolbooks for being myopic, sterile, and useless. But logic made a comeback during the Enlightenment, thanks to René Descartes's *Cogito*, Isaac Newton's mathematical astronomy, and Immanuel Kant's ultimate Reason. And from that time on, logic continued to expand its place in philosophy. In the early nineteenth century, it seeded Romanticism after Georg Hegel revived Aristotle's dialectic, birthing Marxism and the rest of continental philosophy. In the late nineteenth century, it became the basis of analytic philosophy when Gottlob Frege enlarged Aristotle's propositional laws into a calculus that could process any argument. In the early twentieth century, it was leveraged by philosopher-psychologist Charles Spearman into the modern doctrine of "general intelligence," from which we have inherited our faith in critical thinking, creative ideation, and standardized testing. And finally, in the latter decades of the twentieth century, it launched computer AI.

AI is driven by the same syllogisms—AND/NOT/OR—that Aristotle established as logic's immortal laws. Those three syllogisms are hardwired into the logic gates of the computer brain (the Arithmetic Logic Unit, or ALU). And in fact, those syllogisms *are the only rules of thought* that AI—or any computer—ever uses. Which means that the wonders of machine learning all follow the blueprint of the *Organon*. Anything that an algorithm can—or will—think is purest logic.

This is why my teachers didn't associate story with thinking. They'd been impressed by philosophy's wide-ranging epiphanies, from Vedic India to the linguistic turn. They'd learned to measure cleverness as IQ and creativity as design. They'd witnessed the future in AI's electric brilliance. And so, they'd come to equate astuteness with logic and its intellectual fruits, from mathematics to semiotics to computer science; from Euclid's geometry to C. S. Pierce's theory of signs to Alan Turing's proof of general computing; from the political principles of the U.S. Constitution to the hermeneutic methods of the modern humanities to the innovation protocols of divergent and convergent thinking.

What could be wrong with this version of intellectual history? What could my teachers have possibly missed?

WHAT MY TEACHERS MISSED

My teachers weren't wrong to see logic as thinking. They were wrong to see logic as *the only kind* of thinking. That's because there are at least two ways to think: logic and story. Each can solve problems that the other can't; each can create things that the other never will.

This dualism of intelligence can be demonstrated both analytically and empirically.

Analytically, story and logic employ different epistemological methods. Logic's method is equation, or more technically, correlational reasoning, which inhabits the eternal present tense of *this equals that*. Story's method is experiment, or more technically, causal speculation, which requires the past/present/future of *this causes that*. Each method has its own operational range: logic's is stable, high-data environments; story's is volatile, low- (and even no-) data environments. And while there's some overlap between these ranges (e.g., chess, Go, and other board games, at which story can weakly challenge logic; and corporate HR, institutional health care, and other large-scale human systems, at which logic can weakly challenge story), most of what one method can do, the other can't. Story cannot calculate timeless truths; logic cannot generate original actions.

Empirically, story and logic can be traced to different mechanical operations in the human brain. Which is to say, contrary to what many cognitive scientists once believed (and quite a few still do), the brain does not operate like a computer. It operates *partly* like a computer, because some of its neuroanatomical sectors (e.g., the visual cortex) think in representations and other logic functions. But the human brain operates *largely* like a narrative machine, because one of its chief evolved purposes (as evidenced by the antiquity and centrality of its motor regions) is to cogitate in action, and action requires causal speculation, or in other words, storythinking.

This is what my teachers missed. They believed that intelligence could be reduced to a single mechanism. And once they'd equated that mechanism with logic, the only role remaining for story was communication, prompting my teachers to conclude that story's lone job was to transmit logic's inferences to folk who lacked the acumen to be logical themselves.

So confident were my teachers in this conclusion that they overlooked its obvious hitch: story could only communicate *if the brain cogitated naturally in story.* Otherwise, story wouldn't plug with such ease into our gray matter's cranks and pistons. What my teachers had seen as dumbing down was actually story meshing with a main operating system of human intelligence, a system that has helped plot the creative workings of everything from pottery to flying machines, democracy to trade networks, agriculture to antibiotics, scripture to everyday ethics.

Narrative's leading role in human ingenuity doesn't mean that story is the best way to be smart. Our brain evolved blindly, as did everything biological, so there's no enlightened design behind our psychology. Like our epiglottis and our lumbar spine, it's a haphazard mix of luck and legacy, and in the specific case of story, its limits have been exposed not just by the advent of computers (which can marshal their logic gates to identify patterns, run algorithms, and perform other operations impossible for our brain's narrative networks) but also by our own neuroanatomy (which has itself developed a few computational zones, capable of math tasks that story can't accomplish).

Yet narrative's leading role *does* mean that my teachers' logic-based curriculum is shortsighted, for two reasons.

First, by devaluing a major way that we naturally think, it has had deeply negative social consequences. It has institutionalized schoolwork (like the Common Core) that befuddles, shames, and demoralizes students by ruthlessly

9

assessing human brains on tasks—memorization, critical thinking, quantitative reasoning—that are better performed by smartphones and laptops. And it has bred excessive enthusiasm for metrics and data, injecting depersonalization, brittleness, and burnout into our economies, governments, and health care systems.

Second, it overlooks our brain's natural history. That history is riddled with mystery, but even so, we know that our brain's logical circuitry isn't a recent breakthrough that obsolesced story's antiquated mental technology. Far from it: our brain's logical circuitry is itself incredibly ancient, originating more than 500 million years ago in the eye networks of Paleozoic sea swimmers. Logic has thus had plenty of time to make its mark upon the evolution of intelligence; had it outperformed story over the long haul, it would predominate in our head rather than coexisting with storythinking.

These basic facts suggest that smart classrooms, businesses, and cities require more than data-driven decision making, design, and optimization. And they also spur some rebel questions: What if the philosophers had valued story as highly as logic? Would we have middle schools of creative action and PhDs in narrative cognition? Would we have Silicon Valley startups building plot technologies to handle the jobs that flummox computer AI? Would we have more literature and flying machines and democracy and antibiotics?

What problems could we solve—and what innovations could we achieve—if we were better at thinking in story?

GETTING BETTER AT THINKING IN STORY

This book's ambition is to do for storythinking what Aristotle's *Organon* did for logic: provide a philosophical introduction to improving our brain's inborn ability.

This book's ambition, in other words, is to be useful. It won't pretend to diagram story's final truth; truth requires logic's unvarying rules and mathematical landscapes, and story is too supple and provisional for that. It's restricted to good-enough answers to real-world problems. It's an outcast from absolute theory into provisional pragmatism.

Such pragmatism has not, on the whole, proved attractive to philosophers. Even when philosophers attend to praxis (as Aristotle did with rhetoric and William James did later with epistemology), they have a habit, as a wag once wryly observed, of abstracting practice into the *theory* of practice. Yet as intellectually shallow as practicality often feels to the philosophically inclined, it can be a deeply valuable enterprise. Until our lives become a logical utopia—a utopia that, as we'll see in later chapters, is neither possible nor desirable for biological organisms—the mundanities of problem solving and applied innovation will remain the motors of our corporeal survival and mental flourishing.

By improving our storythinking, we can thus make our earthly lives hardier, healthier, and happier. Or to invest that humble project with a loftier tone: *By improving the practice of narrative cognition, we can advance philosophy's original purpose of gaining the good life.* (With "good" understood as "best possible, here and now," and "life" understood as "biological existence, from birth through growth.")

Because of this practical aim, the book you hold is empirical, exploratory, and provisional. Which is to say: it's not ideal, sacred, or immutable. So, nothing you read here will last. It will all be outmoded by future storythinkers, of which one will hopefully be you.

To aid you in that happy task of obsolescence, the following chapters will work to sharpen and extend your innate storythinking skills. The skills are many, but to get the journey under way, the big three are:

(1) **Prioritizing the exceptional.** This is focusing on what's unique, special, and distinct about a person or place (or in narrative jargon, an *actor* or *physical environment*). It's resisting the temptation to abstract individuals into universal archetypes. It's thinking the opposite way from AI, which treats outlying data points as blips, aberrations, noise to be regressed to a statistical mean. It's instead fixating on events that break the pattern of history—and speculating: *What radically new future could they portend?* And it's continuing to speculate again and again, like a library of science fiction novels that unfold different tomorrows, each of which is surprising in the moment but possible in retrospect.

(2) **Perspective shifting.** This is imagining what you'd do if you were someone else, like when you see through a character's eyes in a film or a novel. It comes from identifying a root cause of another person's behavior and internalizing that *why* as your own. Such internalization of outside motives can carry you only so far: it's impossible for your brain to literally become another. Yet it's nonetheless possible to hoist yourself far enough out of your biases, hopes, and fears to productively expand your neural range of action.

(3) **Stoking narrative conflict.** This is encouraging a battle in your head (or in your larger social unit) between two asymmetric physical causes, like when a novelist pits

characters against one another, generating plot. It's different from a conflict between ideas, arguments, theories, and other logical stuff, because instead of generating dialectic syntheses and resolutions, it creates original actions. And the only way to find out what those actions can do is to test them simultaneously, comparing their effects.

These three skills tighten the core mechanism of evolution by natural selection, increasing its creative yield. And all three are performed naturally by your brain. Your brain is wired to notice environmental irregularities (hence, your primal twinges of paranoia); your brain has potent perspective-shifting networks that evolved to see the world from different strategic vantages; and your brain is a democratic conglomerate of individual neurons firing at their own semiautonomous frequencies, generating the constant inner struggles of your storythought.

And just as these mental processes have grown natural selection's root capacity for problem solving and innovation, so too can they themselves be grown.

Through art. And through science.

GROWING STORYTHINKING WITH ART
AND SCIENCE

Historically, our species has grown storythinking via narrative artworks (myths, plays, novels, films) that deploy their own versions of the big three above, tweaking our minds with singular happenings, drawing us into other psychological motives, and crashing together different-acting characters. These three ways of nurturing storythinking

13

can be found throughout global libraries, but as a ready illustration, there's English literature's most celebrated story: *Hamlet*.

(1) *Hamlet* **prioritizes the exceptional.** *Hamlet* focuses our gaze on weird events: bizarre hauntings and unnatural portents; ear poisonings and stairwell burials; revenge machinations so atypical as to seem insane. And it pulls us into the thoughts of a title character who is similarly obsessed with the importance of the unusual: *As a stranger, give it welcome . . . Why seems it so particular to thee? Nay, madam, I know not seems . . .*

(2) *Hamlet* **perspective shifts.** *Hamlet* thrusts us into a litany of alternate psychologies, using innovative techniques such as Hamlet's soliloquies and Ophelia's half-sense songs to prompt our brain to inhabit the purposes of different thinkers.

(3) *Hamlet* **stokes narrative conflict.** *Hamlet* relentlessly collides causal agents, or to use their literary name, dramatic characters: Hamlet against his mother, Hamlet against Polonius, Hamlet against Claudius, Hamlet against Ophelia, Hamlet against Rosencrantz and Guildenstern, Hamlet against Laertes. And also, Hamlet against himself: *To be or not to be . . .*

This three-part recipe is, to borrow the play's own phrasing, "madness . . . [with] method in it." It's the uncertain, unstable, and unpredictable process of imagination rigorized. It's the neural nuts and bolts of how Shakespeare's theater has sparked so many audience members—from Van Gogh to Albert Camus to Maya Angelou—to hatch their own artistic and philosophical creations.

The identical recipe can be found in modern science. To take three quick examples: Charles Darwin's theory of natural selection, Marie Curie's theory of radioactivity, and Albert Einstein's theory of relativity span biology, chemistry, and physics, but they were born of a shared scientific method that hinges on storythinking's big three:

(1) **Science prioritizes the exceptional.** Science emphasizes occurrences that don't fit established models of nature. Darwin was transfixed by the eccentric local beaks of Galapagos finches, Curie by a weird element whose action violated the indivisibility of atoms, and Einstein by the unique properties of light.

(2) **Science perspective shifts.** Science steps into the perspective of natural causes, treating them as actors whose actions can be narrated. Darwin imagined natural selection as a story of too many siblings, Curie imagined molecular reactions as fairy tales, and Einstein imagined himself in footraces with sunbeams.

(3) **Science stokes narrative conflict.** Science pits its hypotheses against one another, honing them into divergent predictions. Because those predictions are narrative, they cannot be arbitrated via logic, only via carefully plotted experiments, like the 1865 pea cross-pollinations with which Gregor Mendel (accidentally) affirmed Darwin, the 1911 gold-foil bombardment with which Thomas Rutherford affirmed Curie, and the 1919 solar eclipse photograph with which Arthur Eddington affirmed Einstein.

Modern science is, in short, Hamlet's laboratory partner. And it's no coincidence that Darwin, Curie, and Einstein all knew Shakespeare's play: Darwin absorbed it as a youthful escape from dreary schoolwork; Curie via the poetry of Polish Romantic Adam Mickiewicz; and Einstein through the theater of Johann Wolfgang von Goethe.

To improve your storythinking, this book will draw upon the same threefold storythinking recipe as narrative art and modern science. Like a biological researcher, it will leap from rogue facts into fresh hypotheses, imagine backward from observed effects to hidden causes, and advance conflicting predictions that can only be resolved via randomized controlled trials. And like a theatrical scriptwriter, it will explore storythinking's past, present, and future through unique characters and their idiosyncratic life narratives. Those narratives will enrich what we've covered in this short introduction by adding new perspectives, twists, and collisions, but their goal is to go beyond communicating knowledge into stimulating original thinking. By immersing you in story's creative processes, they aim to deepen your neural know-how of narrative, like a dance class that deepens a doctor's understanding of anatomy by helping the body act more widely, inventively, and adaptively.

Which is to say, the following narratives won't be stories as my teachers understood them. They won't be rhetorical instruments for implanting deductive typologies, inductive definitions, and interpretive formulas. Instead, they will be tools for cogitating in ways that logic can't. Empowering your brain to strategize in chaos, evolve in doubt, and thrive in life, they will offer methods for the mad.

2

Story and Thinking

A t the dawn of Western philosophy, story was severed
from thinking.

The severance occurred outside of Athens in 335 BCE,
just east of the city's limestone walls. There, at a new-built
library tucked beside a wolf-prowled hill, a wizened polymath unfurled a long papyrus scroll. The polymath was
Aristotle, a Macedonian immigrant who'd spent the past
decade rambling the Mediterranean, studying Egyptian
medicine and Asian flowers. And the long scroll was *The
Republic*. Composed forty years prior by Aristotle's now-dead
teacher, Plato, it chronicled the efforts of Plato's own mentor,
Socrates, to map an ideal government, governed by reason.

To achieve that reason, *The Republic* expelled poetry—
and with it, story. Story was a euphemism for fiction, which
was itself a euphemism for fabrications, deceits, and lies.
And if that wasn't bad enough, story's dramatic fables
churned up unreason's dark enchantment: emotion. To
expunge untruths, feelings, and story's other mental dregs,
the republic's enlightened citizenry therefore outlawed

poets and their myths. In the utopia, there would be mathematics and there would be music. But there would be no narrative.

As Aristotle mulled this political blueprint in the flicker of a seed-oil lamp, he frowned. No narrative? But wasn't *The Republic* itself a story? And weren't Plato's other writings stocked with literary plots, like the tale of Atlantis and the fable of Timaeus? So surely, story wasn't philosophy's enemy. It was instead a humble ally, the easy teacher to philosophy's hard genius. What philosophy reached high into truth's empyrean to pluck, narrative bent low to hand to common understanding.

Pleased with this conclusion, Aristotle inked two scrolls of his own: *Poetics* and *Rhetoric*. In the first, he anatomized how narrative could generate emotion; in the second, how emotion could sway audiences onto the path of reason.

With that pair of insights, Aristotle meant to redeem narrative. But instead, he completed Plato's cutting stroke. From then on, story would be placed by both its detractors and its advocates in the field of learning known as rhetoric, a field sometimes treated as antithetical to philosophy and other times as complementary, but in either case distinct. The philosopher used reason to *think*, while the rhetorician used story to *communicate*.

During the twenty-three centuries since Aristotle, this split between story and thinking has remained characteristic of Western culture, becoming foundational to twenty-first-century law, politics, economics, business, computer science, K–12 education, and even narrative's academic bulwark: literary studies. So deep and omnipresent is the divide that it now seems entirely natural.

But it is not, as we can see by spinning back time's gears to discover how, long before Plato's republic, philosophy's own origin was story.

PHILOSOPHY'S ORIGIN

It was five millennia ago on the silt marshlands of Sumer. Inside the great library at Nippur, where mud-brick gates stood high against the chariot lords, the master taught his students.

He taught how Summer took credit for the June harvest. And how Winter protested, insisting that the harvest soil was fed by January waters. And how the Lord Creator took Winter's side, rebuking Summer's arrogance.

Thus did philosophy begin. Or perhaps not. Perhaps the beginning was elsewhere. Perhaps in Egypt's Twelfth Dynasty, when a scribe claiming to be the reincarnate Ptahhotep handed down the higher prudence: *Do not bully the weak—lest the strong bully you.*

Or perhaps philosophy began in the monsoon foothills of the Himalayas, where the water-drinking Yajnavalkya and his deep-thinking wife mused in the *Brihadaranyaka Upanishad* that the cosmos had been horse-born from hunger's nothingness—and that to know this was to gain wealth, might, and bliss.

Or perhaps in biblical Judah, when dream-seeing King Solomon soared upon his mechanical throne to dictate in Proverbs how everlasting God had separated the firmament with a thoughtful radiance that guided humankind to leave the crooked road and find the Tree of Life.

19

Or perhaps in the paper-roomed Zhou dynasty colleges that Confucius honored in *Analects* for discovering that *ren* was cultivated by "not doing to others what you would not want done to you."

Or perhaps in the Mayan metropolis of Tulan, amid waterfalls and pine, where royal artisans dabbed the *Popol Vuh* on lime-coated strips of deerskin, telling how Sky-Heart implanted Maize men with purposeful eyes.

Or perhaps none of these was the true beginning of *philosophia*. (A Greek term that was unknown to the thinkers above, coined as it was on a faraway Italian shore by the equally faraway psyche of the numerological vegetarian Pythagoras.) Perhaps the beginning was more ancient, indeed, so ancient that it came before any *Homo sapiens*— that synonym for "wise man" with which we self-importantly celebrate our species. Perhaps the beginning happened in a Neanderthal, *Homo erectus*, or other introspective animal, occurring as an unrecorded mental jump that predated human language and its scanty written remnants.

Yet even if the sayings of Confucius, Solomon, Ptahhotep, Yajnavalkya, the royal Mayans, and the Nippur master are more early chapters than true genesis, they nevertheless provide a glimpse of philosophy's first pages. And in those pages, we see: philosophy was not born *ex nihilo* by logic's pure light. Its vast library started as annotations in the margins of another kind of intellectual work: wisdom literature.

Wisdom literature's own earliest days are draped in myth and hearsay, for although wisdom literature came, like philosophy, to be associated with writing's eternal symbols, it was hatched over time by an organic process of oral creation that bore less resemblance to a deliberate sequence of rational choices than to a sprawling garden of vegetable exploration.

This literary garden sprouted (as far as we can tell) from the scattered seeds of many cultures, stretching from the beast fables of archaic Africa and Vedic India to the Near Eastern legends of Genesis and the Book of Job to the otherworldly songs of Amazon prophets and Aborigine Dreamtimers. And what held its branching multiplicity together was not a definable metaphysical essence but a pair of physical processes:

1. A **focus** on answering the question: "How should I live my life?"

This question is the source of the vast philosophical field now known as ethics, and its own source is the brute biological hunger for less pain and more pleasure. That hunger flashed through our animal brain in primordial days, shaping our appetites and yielding the proto-scientific method of trial and error that enabled prehuman hominids to fashion the implements of hunting, fire, and shelter, and our more recent ancestors to craft the tools of agriculture, law, and art.

2. A **method** rich in narrative.

Narrative is actors performing actions. Or in literary terminology, it's characters engaged in plots. Those characters and their plots, like the foundational question of ethics, derive ultimately from our biology, which has evolved to prioritize other humans because they, more than any other environmental factor, determine our worldly success.

We need other humans to solve problems and pass on our genes, and we compete with them over life-sustaining resources, making them not just our friends and lovers but also our rivals and adversaries.

Thus it is that our brain has evolved to function in a human landscape. And thus it is that our brain often narrates that landscape onto the actual geography outside. The sun, the weather, the wheat fields—all are frequently invested by our brain with human motives that manifest in plotted actions: storms reveal their anger through thunderclaps and the wheat fields their creativity through sprouted stalks.

Both features of wisdom literature mark philosophy's earliest works, as we can see by returning to the great library at Nippur and examining the Sumerian tale of Summer and Winter:

The tale's **focus** is practical ethics. By stressing the importance of irrigating the soil many months before harvest, it raises awareness of the benefits of foresight, preparation, and patient labor.

The tale's **method** is heavily narrative. The seasons are anthropomorphized, and their behaviors throw them into conflict, plot's core engine, driving the story forward.

Yet even though the Sumerian tale is wisdom literature, it's not *only* wisdom literature. Already, 5,000 years ago, the focus and the method had begun to undergo a shift that marks the inception of what we now hail as professional philosophy.

THE RISE OF PROFESSIONAL PHILOSOPHY

Professional philosophy is almost as capacious a category as wisdom literature.

It stretches from the Socratic instructors of Plato's Academy to the Islamic academics of the Abbasid Golden Age to the theology faculty of medieval European universities to the metaethics professors of modern higher ed. It doesn't require that philosophers have any specific training or institutional position, but it does require that philosophers exist in enough numbers at any given location to prompt competition over status, students, and tuition. That competition drives philosophers in two related directions. The first is to seek intellectual foundations that can be inured from the attacks of their professional competitors. The second is to develop ways of attacking those competitors back.

The first direction has driven *a shift in focus* from ethics to metaphysics:

> Metaphysics is the search for first principles. It's the hunt for the ultimate cause, the fundamental reason. It is, in other words, an attempt to mount philosophy on the unshakable pedestal known as truth.
>
> Truth is ontologically distinct from action. Action is a going, a growing, or some other doing that changes over time. In the language of philosophy, it's a *becoming*. Truth, in contrast, is *being*. And being is perpetual. It exists forever in the present tense, everlastingly untimed.
>
> Such being is achieved in the Sumerian tale's final moments, where the Lord Creator judges Winter to be

superior to Summer. This superiority isn't temporary, to be undone if Summer wises up or Winter stumbles. It's eternal and absolute, a metaphysical law. It declares that Winter will forever be worshiped over Summer and insists that, even though Summer once usurped Winter, the usurpation was false. The reality, even then, was that Winter was king.

The second direction of professional philosophy has driven *a shift of method* from narrative to argument:

Argument replaces action with equation, identity, interpretation, and other logic-based protocols for relating one state of being to another. And because being exists in the eternal present tense, so does argument. Argument states that X *is* Y, or that X *is* NOT Y. It doesn't state that X *leads to* Y, because such temporal processes are excluded from the eternal.

With this eschewal of change, argument deletes narrative's core function: connecting beginnings to endings, or in other words, describing how specific causes yield specific effects. In the timeless zone of argument, a cause cannot produce an effect, nor can an effect come from a cause. Instead, every cause *is* its effect and every effect *is* its cause: whenever X is present, so is Y. Truth is beauty and beauty truth. Law is justice and justice law.

The result of argument's past-future deletion is to make power symbolic, converting wisdom literature's gods from earthly sources of food, warmth, or light into timeless beings who assert their absolute rightness. Such is the conversion that takes place during the Sumerian tale. The tale begins with the god An planning the day and the god

Enlil copulating with a mountain to engender Winter and Summer (who themselves proceed to birth lambs, butter, honey, and onions). But following these creative actions, the tale switches into timeless arguments. Summer taunts Winter: "Your time *is* chilly, and my time *is* abundant." To which Winter rejoins: "My time *is* strong, and your time *is* filled with clothes-eating moths." The tale then ends with the Lord Creator declaring, "Winter *is* the ruler of life-giving waters." Which the tale then carves into stone by pronouncing: "This verdict *is* unchangeable."

After the Sumerian tale, in the works of Confucius, Solomon, Ptahhotep, Yajnavalkya, and the Mayans, this pivot out of ethics and narrative continued. And as in the Sumerian tale, its result was to invest professional philosophy with more metaphysics—and more argument.

MORE METAPHYSICS, MORE ARGUMENT

In the works of Confucius, Solomon, and other early philosophers, metaphysics doesn't simply become the foundation of ethics. It becomes the *whole* of ethics, from bottom to top.

This transition wasn't driven by a collective program of reform; Confucius, Solomon, and the Mayans had no knowledge of one another. But it *was* driven by an independently shared priority: the seeking of truth. Truth was adopted by philosophers across the ancient world as their common aspiration, an aspiration that, as the philosophers came to recognize, was postponed during, and even disrupted by, the physical pressures of ordinary existence.

Who has time to ponder the world's deep reasons when crops must be planted, watered, and protected from insects? Who hasn't been tempted away from principled pursuits by the material lures of financial profit and social advancement? To create a more capacious and less corruptible space for intellectual questing, the philosophers therefore urged their students to withdraw as much as possible from the jumble and claw of daily survival. Where ethics had served initially as a way of improving the physical health and happiness of farmers and merchants, it thus morphed in early first-millennia-BCE philosophy into an aggrandizement of reclusive sages. Which is why the ultimate lesson of Confucius is: *Be Confucius.* And the ultimate lesson of Solomon is: *Do like me; forget the body's passing troubles to stretch your soul toward eternity.*

This trend accelerated with the rise of professional philosophy and, indeed, was a major reason for the coining and propagation of the term "philosopher." The term means a lover of truth, so when Pythagoras styled himself as such, he implicitly claimed verity as his life pursuit. This equation of ethics with truth seeking was then rendered explicit by Plato, Aristotle, and the many ancient and medieval philosophers (from Plotinus and the Neoplatonists to Ibn Sina and the Islamic Kalāmists to Thomas Aquinas and the European scholastics) who defined the good life as knowing the ultimate facts of Justice and Nature. And its ethos of verity for its own sake remains pervasive in Enlightenment, Romantic, and modern philosophy, leading thinkers as divergent as Descartes, Kant, Hegel, Friedrich Nietzsche, and Martin Heidegger to agree: the highest state of human existence is one spent grappling with the problems of metaphysics.

At the same time that philosophers were transmuting ethics into metaphysics, they were also converting narrative into argument. This conversion can be felt in the allegorical quality of early philosophy, where behaviors (such as kindness) are distilled by Ptahhotep into the truth of *Maat* (eternal heart) and characters (such as the Underworld twins Hunahpu and Xbalanque) are abstracted by Mayan priests into abiding binaries (sun/moon, day/night, light/dark). And the trend accelerated further as philosophy professionalized, as we can see from one of the profession's earliest and most influential works: *Topics*.

Topics was authored in roughly 350 BCE by Aristotle as the fifth book of his *Organon*. Over the previous four books, Aristotle had laid down the rules of induction, deduction, and interpretation, establishing the calculus that would power Catholic theology, Enlightenment science, analytic philosophy, literary semiotics, and digital AI (see chapter 5). Now, in *Topics*, he enriched logic with a tool—dialectic— that would form the foundation of medieval *quaestiones*, Renaissance rhetoric, Hegelian reasoning, Marxism, and modern continental philosophy (see chapter 8).

Dialectic's own basis was Socrates, a stoneworker's son born in 470 BCE Athens, who used his inheritance to establish himself as teacher of young men. One of those young men was Aristotle's teacher, Plato. And after Socrates was executed—really, murdered—in 399 BCE by an Athenian jury, Plato decided to strike back for justice by writing a series of documentary scripts, known as the Dialogues, that preserved Socrates's unconventional approach to truth discovery.

27

That approach was to act like a chatty gadfly: after striking up a conversation with a possessor of strong opinions, Socrates would proceed to query, challenge, and spoof those opinions, precipitating a verbal back-and-forth that midwifed more solidly rational claims.

Impressed by this technique for refining opinion into reason, Aristotle set out, a half-century after Socrates's death, to distill it into a formal argumentative procedure. He set out, in other words, to convert literary *dialogue* into logical *dialectic*. To effect this conversion, Aristotle carefully divested the Socratic Dialogues of their narrative components. The character of Socrates was removed, as was the plot of him talking with Meno, Ion, Gorgias, and other semifictionalized actors, until all that remained was the truth-computing protocol of *thesis-antithesis-synthesis*.

With this purge of narrative, *Topics* completed the reduction of wisdom literature into professional philosophy: a character whose actions modeled a distinctive way of behaving was converted into argumentative propositions that yielded algorithmic outputs. Those outputs, Aristotle was certain, achieved greater rigor than Socrates's narrative chatter, and at no intellectual cost. By replacing story with syllogism, they discarded only rhetorical frippery. Everything of intellectual substance was maintained; none of the thought-machinery was lost.

Yet was this really so? Did *Topics* sacrifice nothing by deleting the nonrational parts of Socrates's psychology? Did it preserve his intelligence entirely intact?

No, it did not. As we can see by expanding our historical lens beyond *Topics*, Aristotle's dialogue-to-dialectic conversion deletes a big part of how Socrates's mind works.

28

HOW SOCRATES'S MIND WORKS

During late antiquity, Socrates's most legendary bit of wisdom was: "I know that I know nothing."

When, where, and even whether these precise words were spoken is unknown: their first record appears in a biography inked by Diogenes Laertius some six hundred years after an Athenian jury sentenced Socrates to death by suicide. But even if the utterance is not literally true, it captures a core element of the Socratic Dialogues. That element is: the plot twist.

Within any given Dialogue, the twist is prepared when we're introduced to a merchant, entertainer, politician, or other successful man-about-Athens. Such men, as evidenced by their worldly achievements, are smart—at least in a practical sense. They know how to make money, woo hearts, and win audiences, so naturally, we find some (perhaps even a lot) of what they say persuasive. It rings true to lived experience; it matches prudent common sense. At which point, it's obliterated. In the plot twist's culmination, Socrates reveals, patiently but irresistibly, that the apparent wisdom of his interlocutors lacks substance, pitching us, the shared thinkers of that insubstantial thought, into the stunned epiphany: *I know less than I thought.* And even: *I'm not sure that I know anything.* Or in other words: *Maybe all I know is that I know nothing.*

This epiphany is self-irony. It's us mentally exiting our perspective to look wryly at ourselves from without. Which is to say: it's a psychological action. It's our prefrontal cortex pointing a perspective-shifting neural network at the rest of our brain.

Because self-irony is an action, it can be processed seamlessly by narrative. Narrative is itself built of action, so a character in a Socratic Dialogue (or any other story) can state, "I know that I know nothing," and the plot continues running smoothly. A glitch occurs, however, when we try to convert that plot—as Aristotle does in *Topics*—into a logical proposition. The propositional form of *I know that I know nothing* is: I KNOW = I KNOW NOTHING, or in other words, X = NOT X. Which is to say, it's a contradiction, a paradox, an incomputable proposition.

Such propositions have a home in mysticism as gateways to God's *via negativa* and other truths beyond rational comprehension. But they must be excluded from formal logic in the way that dividing by zero must be excluded from algebra, for to admit them would be to haywire the system. Thus it is that Aristotle makes the law of noncontradiction a first principle—indeed, *the* first principle—of metaphysics. And thus it is that in *Topics*, Aristotle deletes Socrates's self-irony.

This deletion takes with it a significant chunk of Socrates's psyche. How significant? Well, even if self-irony isn't the essence of Socrates's cerebral activity, it's a major source of his intelligence. It allows him to interrogate his own assumptions, escaping the lazy sophistries that clog less introspective intellects.

And Aristotle's deletion doesn't just eliminate part of Socrates's intelligence. It also eliminates a path for us to develop such intelligence ourselves. That path is the Dialogue's literary plot, which we walk along in our imagination, encountering Socrates as a story character who prompts us to dramatize the mental action: *I know that I know nothing.* (Or to be more technical: encountering Socrates as a causal agent who activates perspective-taking networks in our neo-cortex, stimulating us to act simultaneously as narrative and narrator.)

This process lets us role-play a long-gone philosopher. It helps us grasp his self-ironic cleverness. It allows us to exit our thoughts and test them from an outside vantage.

And that's just the start of the psychological work we can accomplish by walking back Aristotle's logical erasure of plot and character. For by reactivating our neural power to cogitate in narrative, we can go beyond thinking Socratic—and think with many minds.

THINKING WITH MANY MINDS

Socrates wasn't the first Socratic thinker.

Who was first? We can't know for sure. But we do know that self-irony goes back at least two thousand years before classical Athens, all the way to the Sumerian tale of Winter and Summer. At the tale's end, after Winter finishes speaking, Summer experiences a reflexive moment: "Summer thought through it all and calmed down." Here a pre-Socratic character does a Socrates, modeling the use of perspective shifting to examine his own behavior.

And this isn't the only time that the Sumerian tale encourages us to cogitate with another perspective. The tale repeatedly invites us into the thoughts of Summer and Winter: "I groom the plowed fields . . . I gloss fabrics with oils . . . I sweeten drink with cold water." These first-person mental actions aren't the rational introspections of a Greek philosopher, yet they are, no less than self-irony, occasions of narrative perspective shifting. Just like Socrates's *I know that I know nothing,* they activate neocortical networks in our head, nudging us to simulate how the minds of story characters might act. That mental simulation can then be continued by our brain after the tale is finished, sparking real-world thought experiments: *What if I acted like Winter here—or like Summer there?*

Such experiments are hardly rigorous. Winter and Summer are fictional entities without actual psychologies, and even if they did happen to have living brains, we couldn't enter those brains by reading a story. A narrative can do a great deal to our neurons, but it can't convert them into someone else's. No matter how richly or accurately a story depicts another person's thought, the thought is still flashing through our head, which remains forever conditioned by our own subjective memories, traits, and biases. When we imagine ourselves to be acting like Winter and Summer, that's thus exactly what we're doing: *imagining.* There's no irrefutable basis for knowing whether the actions we conjure to mind are the ones that the story characters would take.

Far from invalidating our Winter-Summer thought experiments, however, this imaginary quality is the special opportunity they offer. Returning us to the root meaning of *experiment*—a test of a novel action—it escorts us out of logic's deducible truths into a lab space where we can adopt the role of original actors (or to be technical, original causes) to hypothesize on what might work in practice. Since the biological purpose of this activity is to grow our psychological range of motion, it doesn't matter whether our attempted actions fall within the narrative domain intended by Winter and Summer's Sumerian author. In fact, on a populational level, it's better if we each arrive at slightly different imaginations of what the two characters would do. Such differentiation broadens our collective gamut of mental activity, so that rather than functioning like computers who all reiteratively output the same logical result, our brains follow natural selection in organically branching life's possible actions.

This nonlogical thought process of trial-and-erroring actors and outcomes is narrative cognition. Which is to say: it's storythinking. It's what Aristotle missed by reducing character to communication and thinking to logic. It's an intellectual element of wisdom literature that cannot be reduced to dialectic, syllogistic NOTs and other logical equations. It's an invitation to use imaginative plotting to experimentally expand our brain's breadth of behaviors.

That expansion may add nothing to metaphysics; we may get no closer to the world's ultimate truth by conjecturing the possible actions of Mesopotamian seasons. But such thinking can do something of earthly value: grow our catalogue of daily doings. Or in academic speak: it can contribute to ethics, reconnecting us to the original biological function of the wisdom works that preceded the Sumerian tale and the rise of the professional philosophers.

There's a chance that Aristotle himself realized this. Fifteen years after *Topics*, he authored *Poetics*. And in its knotted paragraphs, he acknowledged narrative's irreducibility to formal logic, perhaps revealing that, as he sat beneath the wolf-prowled hill, he had second thoughts about deleting Socrates from Socratic thinking.

If Aristotle experienced this epiphany, however, it was lost on his philosophical inheritors. They embraced not only the *Organon*'s formalization of logic but also its elimination of narrative, birthing philosophy's golden ages yet

33

simultaneously raising the questions: What if we used philosophy's intellectual rigor not to delete our brain's natural power to cogitate in plot and character—but to sharpen it? Could we advance beyond the early insights of wisdom literature, doing for narrative what the past 2,400 years of metaphysics have done for argument? Could we craft our own *Topics*, our own *Summa Theologica*, our own *Mediations* and *Critique of Pure Reason* and *Phenomenology of Spirit*—but this time for storythinking?

Answers—tentative yet hopefully generative—will be offered by the following chapters. In their pages, we'll see how a more methodical approach to the mechanics of narrative cognition can boost creative intelligence, nurture emotional growth, reform K–12 education, enlarge democracy, and even bring us closer to life's ultimate summit: the meaning of existence.

But to base our inquiry solidly upon first principles, let's begin with the most basic question: Since narrative predates philosophy, what's the story of its own origin?

3

The Origin of Story

The oldest accounts of story's origin come from poets.

Some of those poets were Iroquois tobacco smokers who told how the first stories descended from the holy Lodges of the Sky. Some were Hindu river folk who hymned how the first stories were inspired by Thunder. Some were archaic Peloponnesians—Hesiod, Homer—who sang how the first stories were invented by Calliope and the Muses.

These poetic mythologies charmed many an audience— but exasperated the philosophers, who felt certain that stories had a far less grandiose origin: imitation. Imitation was what primates did when they witnessed something interesting: aped its motions. And the same process of monkey-see, monkey-do, the philosophers assured their students, was the true source of the world's aboriginal stories. Heroic legends and the like weren't heaven-sent inventions. They were facsimiles of earthly happenings. To the extent they contained anything new, it was due not to celestial vision but to embellishment, exaggeration, and other chimpanzee behaviors.

As we'll see in a moment, the philosophers were too quick to dismiss the poets; story may not literally have arisen from divine creators, but it nevertheless traces its initial springs to a primordial mechanism that created—and continues to create—intelligent life. However, before we delve into the science behind the myths of the Sky Lodges, Thunder, and the Muses, let's give the philosophers the respect they denied the poets and see what insights we can glean from their ancient speculations.

The first-known philosophers to plumb story's origin are the fourth-century BCE Greeks Plato and Aristotle. Both claim that the origin is imitation, prompting Plato to condemn story as inauthentic—and Aristotle to celebrate it as a scientific instrument. Aristotle dispenses this surprising tribute in *Poetics* (see chapter 2), where he observes that stories can imitate either the way life literally is or the way life generally works. The former might seem the more intellectually valuable, but Aristotle dismisses it as simple history, devoid of real discernment. It's the latter that yields ethics, psychology, and politics—practical sciences that, while they fall below metaphysics' ultimate peak, still reach the upper slopes of physics.

Why did Aristotle locate this high intelligence in the same tales that Plato rejected as counterfeit copies? He did so because he noticed: stories can possess plausibility. Plausibility is when something sounds like it could be true, even if it isn't actually. This seems dangerous terrain, the hunting grounds of artful dodgers and unscrupulous illusionists. But not according to Aristotle. According to Aristotle, things sound plausible when they imitate the rule of necessity, or in other words, when they stick to the laws of the material world. When a story sounds plausible, it's thus operating like a telescope or a hadron collider: it's shining a light on the mechanics of nature.

Aristotle would be chastised by later philosophers for this equation of plausible stories with natural philosophy. He had himself turned con man, they opined. Or possibly (since he composed *Poetics* in his silver years, long after the logic treatises of his academic prime) gone senile. But Aristotle's equation was merrily embraced by the philosophers' scholarly rivals: the rhetoricians.

The rhetoricians were champions of persuasion. That is, unlike the philosophers, who were most concerned with what *was* true, the rhetoricians were primarily focused on what *seemed* true. This focus prompted the rhetoricians to pay great attention to Aristotle's discovery that story was a source of plausibility. And it wasn't long before one of them leveraged that discovery into becoming the most powerful man in the world.

RHETORIC TAKES OVER THE WORLD

The world's most powerful man was Cicero.

Cicero was born in 106 BCE, two centuries after Aristotle's death. He dedicated his twenties to studying rhetoric. And at the age of forty-three, he achieved the conjuring trick of lifting himself from a nobody clan of southern chickpea farmers into the leadership of Rome's republican empire, its legions so mighty that they'd defeated the elephant knights of Epirus, the gold-palmed princes of Numidia, and even the crucifix oligarchs of Carthage.

Yet it wasn't Rome's military that gave Cicero his global influence. It was that he authored a string of oratorical handbooks—*De Inventione, De Oratore, Ad Herennium*—whose teachings became immensely popular. Over the next two thousand years, those teachings filtered into imperial decrees, underground pamphlets, and theatrical stage plays, swaying the destinies of kingdoms, nations, continents. And their most influential dictum was Cicero's reiteration of Aristotle's claim about story. Or to use Cicero's preferred term for story, *narratio*.

Narratio, Cicero observed when he was a thirty-something trial lawyer, had great persuasive force: whereas bare facts often left juries unconvinced, the same facts incorporated into a story became immediately believable. That believability, moreover, was due to precisely the reason that Aristotle had claimed: story possessed plausibility. By tapping into what seemed intuitively likely to the human mind, it won over audiences by feeling more reasonable than reason, achieving the incredible effect of making true data appear truer.

As evidence of this narrative wizardry, Cicero tirelessly reminded readers of his own most gloriously effective *narratio*, delivered at the dark hour when the republic's freedom was threatened by Cataline. Cataline was a more than usually ambitious senator who in 63 BCE, having failed to rig a popular election, concocted an open power grab: promising debt relief to emeritus soldiers, he raised a mob legion, their ranks hardy with veteran mettle, their cause hardened by financial desperation. All of Rome quaked—but not Cicero. He stepped into the Senate's cramped marble, and facing its huddled mass of nervous legislators, shared a story: "An army is camped outside this city. An army of Romans against the Republic. An army swelling bigger every minute. And two nights ago, its commander—a man who sits among us—yes, I am speaking of you, Cataline! You slipped through the street of the scythe-makers to the home of Marcus Lecca, where you met your accomplices in madness and in wickedness." Such was the power of this Ciceronian narrative that it incited the Senate to expel Cataline, and Cataline to flee to his militia of desperados, and the desperados to panic, abandoning their renegade general to return to their retirement cottages. Soon after, Cataline was dead, massacred alongside his last handful of followers in the frozen grapefields of Pistoia.

Over the succeeding centuries, as Cicero's rhetorical theories permeated Rome's empire, Greek Byzantium, medieval Christendom, Renaissance Italy, Elizabethan England, the intercontinental Enlightenment, and finally, just about every modern college writing course, his equation of story with plausibility became an uncontested truism. Not because of Cicero's writerly eloquence (compelling as it was), but because narrative worked just like he and Aristotle advertised. Politicians, lawyers, entrepreneurs, and students all discovered for themselves: nothing sounds truer to human brains than a story.

Thus it has become that influential talkers—from Barack Obama to Sheryl Sandberg to the next salesperson you encounter—are practiced storytellers. MBAs at Harvard, the globe's most successfully self-promotional business school, are scrupulously instructed: "Telling a story has been proven to be a superior way of communicating information because people process stories differently than they do non-narrative information, such as a simple recitation of facts."

None of this has done much to shift the thinking of philosophers. Most have continued to agree with Aristotle's critics: story's rhetorical potency makes it as readily a tool of falsehood as of scientific accuracy. Meanwhile, the handful of philosophers who've sided with Aristotle have also typically followed the Greek in viewing narrative as derivative of the world's underlying physics, a mental mirror of material reality.

Few philosophers today, that is, take seriously the poets' old claim that narrative is a god work, or to phrase it in less high-flown speech, that narrative creates original possibilities for thinking and doing. Yet more philosophers should. Because the plausibility that Aristotle detected in storytelling reveals that story's origin goes far deeper than imitation, all the way down to a life-making source of new actions, new actors, and even new worlds.

THE DEEPER ORIGIN OF STORY

Buried inside the worldly success of Cicero's rhetorical maxim is a mystery: *Why* is storytelling so powerful? Why has narrative long been recognized—by even its detractors—as a potent mode of communication? Why do human brains absorb stories better than raw facts and figures?

To Aristotle, the mystery had a clear solution: the world was eternal. Aristotle reached this answer via logic, which (as we saw in chapter 2) makes everything perpetual, leading the Greek to conclude that since the eternal laws of physics were expressed through actions, it was only natural that the human psyche should contain an equally eternal, action-learning mechanism. That mechanism, Aristotle deduced, was imitation, which he viewed as the soul's inborn tool for converting observed, external doings into mental, inner narratives.

This explanation for storytelling's potency has been upended by modern science, which by replacing Aristotle's everlasting cosmos with the shifting environments of natural selection has reopened the mystery of why our brain finds spoken narratives so plausible. Those narratives, as any biologist will tell you, were absent from the ecosystems in which our brain evolved. Before archaic humans invented speech, there existed no anecdotes, no personal histories, no Aesopian fables. There were only bits of information, input to the brain from eyes and ears and other senses. Such sensory data has thus been processed by the animal brain for hundreds of millions of years, while oral stories have been processed for less than one percent of that period, meaning that logically, the brain should have evolved many more neural systems for crunching megabytes than for running narratives. Yet somehow the opposite is true. Why? Why are our primeval mechanisms of intelligence so adept at the nascent communication technology of story?

The answer is: our brain is good at processing the narratives of Cicero and other orators because even though story is an evolutionarily modern method of *communication*, it's an evolutionary ancient method of *thinking*. As we can see by going back to life's beginnings.

At those beginnings, the sea was scattered with bobbing life-forms. The life-forms came in multiple varieties, from grifting virus particles to nitrogen-feasting microbes to sun-catching bacteria. But their diversity was still just subcategories of bobbing. None of it chased food or evaded danger; it all acquiescently floated where the waves went, borne by the whims of the current.

Until one day, more than a billion years ago, action evolved. Its earliest manifestation was probably a primitive flagellum, an ancestor of the whiplike appendage that now propels human spermatozoa. But whatever action's first anatomy, it gave life an opportunity to shape the future. No longer did our microscopic ancestors need to trust entirely to the luck of slipstreams. They could paddle forward destiny.

That fate-changing motion wasn't intentional in the sense of being consciously planned, but as millennia passed, it did become increasingly responsive to feedback. Life would flail its limbs in one direction, and when the flailing had a beneficial outcome, it would be repeated. The result was a creative process through which random improvisation and positive reinforcement combined to produce adaptive learning, learning that took a leap forward with the evolution of a new cell type: the neuron.

The neuron's earliest beginnings are shrouded in obscurity. All we know is that one day, more than 525 million years ago, the neuron caused a tail to flick, a mouth to close, or a body to turn. It did so by committing an action, or as scientists now call it, an *action potential*: an electrical transmission that jumps down the neuron's axon, from dendrites to synapses.

Like the flagellum, the neuron thus evolved a capacity for behavior, conditioned by feedback in response to blind spontaneity. Such spontaneity is embedded in the neuron's biology; unlike an electronic wire, which transmits only when triggered, a neuron pulses continuously at its own idiosyncratic frequency, a frequency that can be regulated by other neurons but can't (unless the neuron is killed) be dialed down to zero. To be a neuron is therefore necessarily to possess some independent activity. In contrast to a computer circuit, a neuron isn't the mathematically derived sum of its inputs but is always informed in part by inner impulse.

That impulse allows neurons to do more than mule-train data; it allows them to initiate activity, which in turn enables them to pilot their own experiments. Neurons can fire wildly and after being informed of the result, can calibrate the firing, learning to operate within productive bandwidths.

At first, the neurons who engaged in this experimental behavior did so solo. They were lone mad scientists, shooting out arbitrary actions to a minimal limb and receiving input from a simple sense organ (perhaps even the limb itself). Until neurons discovered: they could network. And by networking, they could experiment more widely—and more responsively.

THE NEURON NETWORKS

Neural networks were made possible by the evolution of the synapse.

The synapse was originally the junction between a neuron and a motor cell. That junction took the form of a chemical-mechanical prod through which the neuron affected the non-neuron's behavior (for more detail, see chapter 6). But roughly 500 million years ago, the synapse developed into a tool for one neuron to affect another, making possible the first nervous systems and with them, the origins of the animal brain. From there, the synapse branched and evolved into an astonishing variety of machineries that—through intricate protein operations— enable neurons to increase or decrease each other's activity (an influence that primarily runs from synapse to dendrite but can also flow in the opposite direction).

The upshot of those operations is that synaptic networks can generate experimental action scripts that in turn generate physical doings: two muscles (or two hundred) can contract in orchestrated sequences, allowing bird wings to fly, cheetah eyes to stalk, and human fingers to type on keyboards. With such doings, the synapse enlarges the innovation engine of natural selection. Natural selection operates by hatching functional variants that are winnowed by the environment. Neural networks do the same, with a twist: their functional variants aren't reproducible organisms, they're reproducible *behaviors*. This way, adaptation can happen faster; instead of requiring the generation of new bodily structures, it can discover new operations for already existing anatomies.

Or put simply, neurons are the source of the mental marvel that we know as creativity. Creativity gets its name from "creation," which is what natural selection does: generate original organisms. Neurons build upon that process by generating original actions that allow animals to increase their odds of biological success. Those original actions aren't, biologically speaking, inheritable (although we humans have devised cultural methods, such as schools and art, to bequeath them to later generations). But even if animals can't pass their survival-boosting innovations to their offspring, they can still pass along the genetic capacity to make such breakthroughs. Which is why, over hundreds of millions of years, some animal brains have evolved to become more effectively imaginative, enlarging the root power of neuronal creativity.

Neuronal creativity isn't autonomous in the metaphysical sense of possessing free will. It's a physical operation that can happen without sentience—and so without intention. But neuronal creativity *is* autonomous in the practical sense of being liberated from what the brain has done before. It can be as wildly original as the world's first heartbeat, vocal cord, or opposable thumb, powering limbs on journeys never taken before.

Because neuronal creativity takes the form of original action, it exists physiologically as narrative sequences of *this causes that*. Which is why creativity manifests in our consciousness as storythinking. Storythinking is our brain riffing up new chains of actions. It's us planning original deeds, speculating on the future effects of present doings, hypothesizing on the causes of observed occurrences, and generally imagining what might happen and why. It's the superpower that has allowed our species to adapt like no other, inventing the extraordinary life improvements of culture, science, business, and technology. It's a major reason that you and I are alive today, and it's our tool for plotting better tomorrows.

So, from a modern scientific perspective, Aristotle was partly correct about story. Even though his metaphysics prioritized logic as the timeless stuff of true intelligence, he saw that the physical world and much of human psychology ran on action. Meanwhile, the poets—Iroquois, Hindu, and Greek—were even more right. They realized that story could go beyond imitation into creation. Like a deity, it could generate original doings that made living things resilient, adaptive, and ever branching.

That solves the mystery of why our brain is so good at cogitating in narrative. The answer being: because life is sustained by creative action. And creative action isn't derived, logically, from data. It comes about nonlogically through trial and error. A trial and error that occurs insentiently as synaptic improvisation and sentiently as storythinking.

Yet this answer, like the answers before, raises new questions: If storythinking is a source of creative action, and if creative action is a biological wellspring of innovation, problem solving, and resilience, then why is this little book the first time you've heard of storythinking? Why isn't narrative cognition a subject taught to all of us in school? Why aren't we trained to get more out of our plot-hatching brains, helping us imagine more widely, sustainably, and successfully?

Why are we so relentlessly drilled, from kindergarten to college, to think not in story but in logic?

4

Why Our Schools Teach Logic, Not Story

The day broke hot and overcast. But at the United States Department of Education, the teachers smiled cool and sunny for the cameras.

The date was June 2, 2010. And the beaming teachers were spearheading a pedagogical initiative that traced its origins to the 1990s, a decade that America's leaders had begun by giddily reveling in the Soviet Union's collapse—and had ended by fretting that their own superpower would topple next. If the United States were to remain atop the global pecking order, its schools had to crank out the world's smartest young scientists, soldiers, bankers, engineers, and policy makers. Yet there was already a troublesome sign that things were trending oppositely: high school test scores in reading and math were sagging in comparison to European and Asian countries. To win the intelligence war, the United States therefore vowed to undertake bold educational reform, starting with a cutting-edge K–12 curriculum.

The result was presented that day in Washington, D.C. Known as the Common Core, it took what the bright, air-conditioned teachers saw as the progressive side of a debate that had erupted in 1880s England. At that time, the British Empire was at its peak, but just as in 1990s America, concern had arisen about the best way to train young minds to maintain the empire's wealth and influence.

On one side was the Oxford classicist and school inspector Matthew Arnold, who endorsed the traditional pedagogy (stretching back through Renaissance humanists to Byzantium schoolmasters and Greek Sophists) of steeping students in epic poems, theatrical plays, and other literary narratives. Those narratives, Arnold was certain, instilled culture, which was to say, the right way to think and act; for, as Sir Philip Sidney had deftly argued in his 1580 *Defense of Poetry*, literature combined history's vivid particularity with philosophy's virtuous generalities, making it a pleasant stair to moral truth.

On the other side was the self-educated comparative anatomist Thomas Henry Huxley, who believed that the future lay in new forms of the practical arts—commerce, industry, medicine—outlined in the 1620s by Sir Francis Bacon in his visionary *New Atlantis*. Rather than immersing students in the Shakespearean masterworks championed by Arnold, Huxley favored a focus on the newer academic areas of science, technology, engineering, and mathematics—or STEM, as they would later be summed.

America's Common Core teachers agreed with Huxley, front-and-centering STEM in their new curriculum. By doing so, they limited the space for Shakespeare and other literary stories, which, you might think, is why American students don't learn to storythink in school today. But in fact, from the perspective of storythinking, the Core's emphasis on STEM wasn't the problem. The problem was what the Core did with the literary stories it retained.

It retained those stories under the heading "Language Arts." The heading was uncontroversial. None of the teachers in D.C. had any doubts about its appropriateness, and with good reason: it reflected the overwhelming consensus of middle school, high school, and college literature instructors across America (and for that matter, Europe). The only complaint came from a contrarian faction so minuscule in its numbers—and so utterly out of step in its thinking—that it seemed a typical instance of the rule-proving exception.

The out-of-step faction contained the remnants of a scholarly movement that had begun in the 1930s at the University of Chicago's literature department but failed to catch on elsewhere. By the era of the Common Core, the ranks of this "Chicago School" had dwindled to a smattering of U.S. academics, yet refusing to go entirely silent, its remaining members raised the question: Why was the Core treating literary works as *Language* Arts instead of as *Narrative* Arts? Or to put it more directly: Why was Shakespeare being analyzed as semantics rather than as story?

The question was regarded by the Core's architects as bizarre, even perverse. To them, the answer was obvious: narrative was composed of language. This followed deductively from (1) the incontestable fact that Shakespeare's stories were printed on play scripts as words; and (2) the equally incontestable fact that words were language.

Yet as self-evident as all this was, there remained something to the Chicago School's question. For by treating stories as nothing more than language, the Common Core had done just as the Chicago School had charged. It had deleted narrative.

THE COMMON CORE'S DELETION OF NARRATIVE

The deletion's origins go back to Cambridge (later, Harvard) University literature professor I. A. Richards.

Richards was not one of the teachers in D.C. He'd passed away thirty years earlier, in 1979, while America was more worried about Soviet nukes than Chinese STEM. But still, it was Richards who provided the justification for the Core's decision to opt for "Language" over "Narrative," a justification he'd developed by turning to logic, or to be precise, to the subfield of logic known as semiotics.

Semiotics is the application of symbolic logic to language. It was pioneered in roughly 350 BCE by Aristotle's *On Hermeneutics*, another book in the *Organon* (see chapter 2). Since those early days, it has grown to encompass a range of competing theories, yielding viewpoints that are famously—even infamously—diverse. Yet even so, its roots in symbolic logic lend it (and all its hermeneutic offspring) a broadly consistent methodology. That methodology is to treat texts as sets of propositions that establish equations (i.e., identities) between subjects and predicates (e.g., man = the rational animal). Those propositions are then crunched via Aristotelian logic's three syllogistic rules—AND, OR, NOT—to yield truth statements that reveal what the texts are claiming, or more colloquially, what the words mean.

When transferred onto written narratives, semiotics has three broad consequences:

1. It treats novels, plays, fables, epic poems, films, and other stories as collections of symbols. These symbols are, most basically, the words found on printed pages. But they're often also extended to include poetic images and cultural representations that are taken to signify ideas, attitudes, trends, and social groups.

2. It converts literature into a vehicle for truth claims. Those claims can be about nature, human psychology, society, ethics, metaphysics, or anything. But because they're statements about what is TRUE and FALSE, they often pertain to what is RIGHT and WRONG, stretching into ideology and morality.

3. It derives (2) from (1) via a logical technique known as interpretation. That is, after identifying a story's key symbols, semiotics uses interpretation to transform those symbols into arguments, themes, allegories, motifs, and other propositional forms of meaning.

Interpretation has a wide-ranging history that extends beyond the formal semiotics of Aristotle's *On Hermeneutics* to incorporate Bronze Age Indian commentators from the *Rigveda*, Zhou dynasty compilers of the *Shijing*, gnostic commentators on the Hebrew Bible, and Aesop in his beast fables. But these alternate traditions all follow the same basic 3-2-1 process of converting narratives into symbolic meanings. And in the case of I. A. Richards, his 3-2-1 derived directly from the semiotic mainstream.

That mainstream flowed from a fourth-century epistle (composed in a cave under the Bethlehem hills) in which the Christian theologian Saint Jerome articulated *de optimo genere interpretandi*—"the best method of interpreting." It merged with Aristotle's logic in the medieval universities of Europe, where diligent friars wielded syllogisms to distill *Beowulf, Oedipus,* and *The Aeneid* into moral allegories. It was reenergized in the nineteenth century by a pair of influential logicians, Ferdinand de Saussure (1857–1913) and C. S. Peirce (1839–1914). And when it came to Richards's attention in the early 1920s, he became convinced: semiotics was the only rationally valid way to analyze literature.

Indeed, so utterly rational and so utterly valid was semiotics, in Richards's opinion, that it necessitated a purge of what was then the era's most popular approach to literary studies, an approach known as character criticism.

Character criticism wasn't logical. It was narrative. It had its roots in the human brain's biological interest in the origins of other people's behaviors (see chapter 2). This interest had prompted seventeenth-century theater audiences and eighteenth-century novel readers to ask *why* dramatic characters acted as they did, and it was subsequently mobilized by nineteenth-century German Romantics (such as A. W. von Schlegel) and English Victorians (such as A. C. Bradley) to minutely anatomize the doings of Hamlet, Lady Macbeth, and other literary persons. The anatomizing worked via causal thinking: after isolating a character's public actions, character criticism hypothesized private motives beneath.

The resulting speculations were by no means unanimous; wildly divergent motives were ascribed to Hamlet by different scholars, performers, and members of the general public. But character criticism's overall method was so uncontroversial as to be ubiquitous, and it reigned unchallenged in Europe's lecture halls and book clubs—until I. A. Richards used semiotics to prove: character criticism had a shortcoming.

A shortcoming that reflected an intractable problem with narrative itself.

NARRATIVE'S INTRACTABLE PROBLEM

The problem is narrative's relationship to data.

Data is logic's lifeblood. It flows into the veins through induction, is pumped around by deduction, and oxygenates the muscles of argument, interpretation, and critical thinking.

No such data connection exists in narrative. Narrative can jump past the facts, as in imaginative speculation. It can run free of verities, as in literary fiction. It can even flatly contradict the truth, as in counterfactual thinking.

This independence from data is the source of narrative's creative powers. It's why narrative can shake free of the ways things *are* to invent what *could happen*. It's why narrative can chart fresh paths and original tomorrows. It's why narrative can remake the world instead of being predetermined by it.

But this independence from data is also the genesis of untold distortions of reality, via elision, bias, and outright fabrication. Such distortions litter the book you hold now. In this chapter, the narrative has glibly lumped the Common Core teachers into a single grinning entity, when those teachers were different people with diverse perspectives and professional experiences. In the previous chapter, the narrative presented storythinking as the culmination of an evolutionary process of neuronal development—when natural selection is a blindly insentient process without any direction. And in the chapter before that, the narrative

53

flashed inside Aristotle's head to reveal what he was thinking—when the narrative was simply guessing.

This looseness with facts is what hatched Plato's original attack on story (see chapter 2). And it similarly motived I. A. Richards to reject character criticism. Character criticism had been deployed by the Romantics to conclude that the cause of Hamlet's unique behavior was his mental habit of "abstracting" (i.e., of overthinking). But the only evidence for this conclusion was a single word—"abstract"—deployed once by Hamlet during a singular conversation with his girlfriend's offbeat father. That was not data, not by logic's standards. It was a sample size of one, the very definition of statistical insignificance. Hardly surprising, then, as Richards pointed out, that early twentieth-century literary studies was not considered a "real" scholarly discipline with the rigor of mathematics or the moral sciences. Indeed, so scholastically peripheral was literary studies that it wasn't part of Cambridge University's official budget, forcing Richards to collect tuition from his students as they filed into the classroom.

Semiotics allowed Richards to escape this embarrassingly subordinate status, upgrading literary studies into a logical apparatus with the hallmarks of calculus and analytic philosophy. Semiotics insisted that literature's fundamental stuff wasn't characters and their actions; it was words and their meanings. To deduce those meanings, semiotics taught readers to convert narratives into symbols—then to interpret those symbols for propositional content. Richards called this "close reading," and to his students at Cambridge, it seemed a revelation. What semiotics had done to the Bible's chapters and verses, close reading did to *Hamlet*, converting printed text into a font of hidden truth statements.

Close reading's logical method took hold of higher ed with incredible speed. After being elaborated by Richards in *The Meaning of Meaning* (coauthored with C. K. Ogden in 1923), *Principles of Literary Criticism* (1924) and *Practical Criticism* (1929), it gained a devoted following among a crew of midcentury transatlantic scholars who styled themselves the New Critics. The New Critics became highly influential in postwar America, publishing popular textbooks (such as John Ransom's 1941 *The New Criticism* and Cleanth Brooks's 1947 *The Well-Wrought Urn*) and rising steadily through the academic ranks: in 1979, Yale appointed a New Critic as its president; in 1991, Harvard did the same.

And although New Criticism was challenged from the 1970s onward by new theoretical paradigms— deconstruction, psychoanalysis, new historicism—none of them disputed Richards's core claim: that literary narratives were composed of words, representations, and other symbolic stuff that could be analyzed to yield propositional content. Even as literary studies absorbed an eclectic array of hermeneutics drawn from history, critical theory, Marxism, cognitive science, and other academic fields, those hermeneutics were all used to assert (or critique) what literature was saying (overtly or implicitly). While scholars vigorously disagreed about *how* literature should be interpreted, their disagreement thus tacitly united them in a deeper consensus: *that* literature should be interpreted.

This consensus held together literary studies as it fractured over the twentieth century (just as biblical hermeneutics had fractured over the sixteenth century) into competing sects whose shared anchoring in semiotics enabled them to claim that beneath their irresolvable disputes were a set of practical intellectual skills. In addition to

55

interpretation (which allowed readers to extract the meanings of written texts, historical facts, physical gestures, political statements, scientific claims, and other data points), there was also *argument* (which was produced by weighing and debating different interpretations) and *critical thinking* (which came from identifying the logical flaws of biased or hasty interpretations).

In 2010, that scholarly consensus became the basis of the Common Core. The Core explicitly mandated that the Language Arts would develop "critical thinking" by teaching students to "read closely." This was I. A. Richards's "close reading," tactfully rephrased to reach beyond New Criticism into broader methods of textual analysis. And like Richards and those broader methods, the Core stressed logic, interpretation, argument, and data-backed reasoning:

> Read closely to determine what the text says explicitly and to make logical inferences from it; cite specific textual evidence when writing or speaking to support conclusions drawn from the text.
>
> Interpret words and phrases as they are used in a text, including determining technical, connotative, and figurative meanings, and analyze how specific word choices shape meaning or tone.
>
> Delineate and evaluate the argument and specific claims in a text, including the validity of the reasoning as well as the relevance and sufficiency of the evidence.

Thus were the faults that Richards had detected in narrative deleted, upgrading American education and upholding the nation's global ascendance.

Or so the United States Department of Education convinced itself. But the department had placed too much faith in Richards's method. By replacing narrative with semiotics, the Core may have rendered literary coursework more logical, yet the result wasn't to make the US school system unequivocally better. Instead, it was to deprive students of literature's full educational benefits.

WHAT SEMIOTICS MISSES

By exchanging narrative for logic, semiotics deletes a great deal of what poetry, fiction, and theater can teach, as becomes clear when we turn back before Richards to the origin of literature.

That origin, according to semiotics, is the Latin word *litterātūra*, which literally means "that which is lettered," or in other words, "that which is writ." But prior to being writ, literature was oral. Printed texts and their alphabet letters came later, as a way of recording the dramatic performances of poets, playwrights, and mythmakers. So, it's worth asking: Was anything lost in the recording?

We can answer this question by excavating the anthropological origins of writing. Writing was invented (in multiple cultures, independently, more than five thousand years ago) as a record-keeping aid for merchants who wanted to log commercial transactions, regents who wanted to document political treaties, and priests who wanted to maintain ancient rites and rituals. Writing came to be, in other words, as a *memorial* tool. It was devised not as a standalone representation of reality but as a prompt to help human brains recall things. Those things included objects and events, so writing developed nouns and verbs, respectively. Yet beneath nouns and verbs' shared linguistic nature was a functional difference: nouns referred to things that needed only space to exist, whereas verbs referred to things that required time.

This difference matters because writing (like any symbol system) does not exist in time, only in space. So, nouns can embody objects in a way that verbs cannot embody events. You can visualize the distinction by rewinding history before the development of alphabets, returning writing to its archaic beginnings in etched and painted pictures. A picture can capture objects such as trees and humans, but a picture cannot capture events such as a tree growing or a human running. To depict those actions requires *two* pictures, the first with a shorter tree and the second with a taller; the first with a person's legs in one position and the second with the legs advanced. Yet even those two pictures don't capture the event's physical action; the action occurs in the gap between them. And if we fill that gap with a third picture, we still don't capture the action. Instead, we create two more gaps where the action occurs, unseen.

If the action cannot be captured on the page, then where does it exist? The answer is: It exists in a human brain that reads the page. The brain's narrative machinery thinks in action, so it can reconstitute the element of time by remembering tree growing, leg running, and other physical motions signaled by verbs. And indeed, our brain's machinery does this so automatically that it never occurs to most of us that the narrative is not contained in the printed text of books and scrolls. The narrative appears to be self-evidently there, explaining the intuitive but faulty belief that Shakespeare is merely language.

This faulty belief had no practical consequence when Shakespeare was read by nineteenth-century character critics, because their storythinking neurons ran unhampered by their conscious conviction that *Hamlet*'s script fully reproduced the playwright's physical imagination. A gigantic glitch occurred, however, when Richards fed the script into semiotics and its logical apparatus. That apparatus lacked a narrative mechanism for recalling the action absent from the script's static symbols. It could only read those symbols for what they literally were, remaining oblivious to the story elements—actors, events, dramatic conflicts—that the script's verbs had been intended to prompt in the brains of human readers.

Even though Richards claimed to be analyzing literature more rigorously, he was thus missing most of its original ingredients. And likewise, even though the Common Core emphasized the "extensive reading of stories, dramas, poems, and myths," it was really only skimming. By converting literature into language and then interpreting language with semiotics, America's futuristic curriculum was flattening four-dimensional narratives into two-dimensional propositions that reduced characters to representations and plots to arguments. Behaviors became themes, happenings became meanings, and actions became allegories, expunging much of the psychological activity that Shakespeare and the rest of our global library had been crafted to generate.

And there you have the answer to the question posed at the last chapter's end: Why aren't we taught storythinking in school? Storythinking requires stories, and over the past century, our educational institutions have programmatically erased the story from the world's most powerful myths, plays, novels, memoirs, films, comics, and television series, just as the philosophers did to wisdom literature five millennia before (see chapter 2).

All of which would be entirely salutary if Richards and the philosophers were right to think that data-driven logic is the lone mental tool required for a wise and prosperous life. But as we'll explore in the following chapter, it's not.

5

The Limits of Logic—or Why We Still Need Storythinking

Among the schizophrenics of the German Reich, the epiphany struck: *mental illness was a breakdown of logic*.

The epiphany fired the young doctor into ecstasy. And soon the ecstasy would spread, sparking epiphanies even more incandescent:

> The insanities of society—war, injustice, poverty—could be fixed by a more logical mind.
> That more logical mind was the smarter version of the human brain known as "the computer."
> The computer would learn to invent more of itself, until everywhere was a rational heaven.

This was a utopian vision to rival any in history, a vision that would come to be known in the later twentieth century as the Singularity. And to many hopeful souls, over many faithful generations, it seemed the true religion. Yet unfortunately, the epiphanies—all of them—were errant.

They were errant because they rested on the belief that intelligence can be reduced to logic, and logic, powerful as it is, can only compute what *is*, not what *could happen*. It can only understand the future as a version of the past, so it can only survive inside board games, mathematical simulations, medieval theologies, planned communities, rigged economies, and other artificially bounded environments with never-changing rules. It cannot react to change, adapt to emergent threats, exploit fresh opportunities, cope with uncertainty, handle instability, innovate, or grow.

This operational limit to logic is why computer AI can defeat humans at chess—but not write novels, innovate technology, or do scientific research. And it's why the Core Curriculum and the other educational reforms described in the previous chapter are misdirected. By emphasizing memorization, evidence-based reasoning, critical thinking, design, and other logical skills, those reforms teach students to operate like computers. But for humanity, that's a double loser.

First, we humans will never out-compute computers. Their silicon circuits are already better at logically crunching data than we'll ever be, so why devote the bulk of school time to setting up future generations to be second-class algorithms?

Second, by focusing on teaching logic, we're neglecting human intelligence's main source: the plan-generating, hypothesis-imagining, action-inventing neural processes of storythinking. We're leaving young minds unprepared to cope with a tomorrow that demands creative problem solving, innovation, and all the other narrative actions that computers can't do. It makes as much sense as drilling a child for twelve years in basic addition, then handing her a calculator and telling her to cure cancer. What she knows, her tool knows better; what she needs, she hasn't been equipped to accomplish.

If you're confident about all this—if you already know that humans, unlike computers, are capable of nonlogical, non-magical thought that enables adaptation and innovation—then skip to the next chapter, where we'll explore the brain machinery that powers storythinking, launching us on a journey to discover how that machinery can be upgraded by a different educational approach that culminates not in AI autocracy but in human democracy.

But if you suspect otherwise—if you think that logic could solve all the world's problems, that the future lies in design thinking, or that computers will someday replace us—then here's the story of the young doctor and his epiphany.

THE YOUNG DOCTOR'S EPIPHANY

The young doctor was Eilhard von Domarus.

Domarus was born on October 12, 1893, in the German Empire's Kingdom of Saxony, where he survived the Great War to train in neurology at the University of Jena. In 1922, he traveled to the Rhine city of Bonn to work at a psychiatric clinic, which housed, in underfunded and desperate conditions, patients suffering from hysteria, trench trauma, and schizophrenia. To Domarus's dismay, none of the psychic treatments he'd faithfully memorized in school did anything to heal his patients. So, turning his back on the failed panaceas of past generations, he ventured east, across the Bauhaus jazz cabarets of the Weimar Republic, searching for new medicine.

In Freiberg, he imbibed philosophy under the logical idealist Edmund Husserl and the hermeneutic ontologist Martin Heidegger; in Berlin, he studied Gestalt psychology under Wolfgang Köhler and Max Wertheimer; until finally he began, under the Platonist turned empiricist Carl Stumpf, to swirl together all he'd learned, dreaming of a future science that would link human reason to precise neuroanatomical mechanisms. That science would enable doctors to troubleshoot the nervous systems of shell-shocked veterans. That science would turn lunatics into true philosophers. That science would root out the neurological misfires responsible for hatred and violence.

These ideas, spectacular as they were, went generally unheeded. Until in 1930, Domarus earned a fellowship to do a PhD across the Atlantic at Yale University. And at Yale, he encountered a mind as unusual as his own.

The second unusual mind was possessed by Warren Sturgis McCulloch. Born into a pious New Jersey household in 1898, young McCulloch entertained thoughts of becoming a minister, going so far as to journey in his late teens to study with Philadelphia's Quakers at Haverford College. But while still in his freshman year, he heard echo through the sacred pastures: *Whiz! Boom! Bang!* It was the Great War, raging across France. And coming to believe that this industrial conflict—with its machine guns, field radios, and portable X-rays—was a harbinger of scientific innovation, McCulloch quit his pacifist teachers and enrolled in 1918 as a trainee naval officer at Yale.

Yale had no sooner welcomed McCulloch into its wood-paneled classrooms than the combat in Europe ended. But McCulloch found another outlet for his futurism in the emergent laboratory discipline of psychology, which offered curious minds the chance to upgrade humanity in a less bellicose, more clinical fashion. After picking up a major in philosophy and minor in psychology, McCulloch headed postgraduation to Columbia University, earned a psychology master's and a medical degree, then returned to do neurophysiology research at Yale. And there, amid a building boom financed by the collapsing wage structure of the Great Depression, McCulloch met Domarus.

The two doctors quickly bonded over their shared conviction that philosophy and psychology were poised to converge. As formulated by McCulloch: "What is a number, that a man may know it, and a man, that he may know a number?" Or summed up even more concisely by Domarus: *sanity = logic*.

Eager to arithmetic further, McCulloch spent the early 1930s helping Domarus translate his PhD thesis from a complicated cacophony of German, Greek, Latin, and English into a book on the "logical structure" of healthy human cognition. The book would later be published with the support of NASA and the U.S. Air Force, and sensing further triumphs in the future they were co-creating, the two unusual minds traveled upstate to New York's Rockland Asylum, where McCulloch delved into the electronics of epilepsy while Domarus patiently explained the finer points of deductive reasoning to the inmates.

Hung up on the belief—dubbed the "von Domarus principle"—that schizophrenia stemmed from a brain hitch in processing the middle term of syllogistic propositions, Domarus gently faded into obscurity. But his conviction that human brains were logic processors endured in McCulloch as he blazed a singular path across the academic firmament. In the later 1930s, McCulloch entered

Yale's Institute of Human Relations to attend the seminars of Clark L. Hull, who, inspired by Bertrand Russell's recent reduction of math to logic, was determined to do the same to the psychological sciences. Then in 1941, after funding dried up at Yale, McCulloch relocated to the University of Illinois at Chicago, which provided a lab for him to test his (later debunked) theory that toxic doses of insulin could shock schizophrenics into thinking logically.

And in Chicago, McCulloch encountered another unusual mind. The most unusual of them all.

THE MOST UNUSUAL MIND

The mind belonged to Walter Pitts.

Pitts was a vagrant autodidact who in 1935, at the age of twelve, had huddled in a Detroit public library for three straight days, poring over Bertrand Russell's coauthored magum opus, *Principia Mathematica*. Captivated by the work's intricate density but troubled by what he perceived as its lack of rigor, the precocious youth sent Russell a letter listing the *Principia*'s computational shortcomings. Impressed, Russell invited Pitts to study logic with him at Cambridge University—an offer that Pitts declined. Trusting instead to his own intelligence, Pitts returned to the public library, imbibing logic's first truths from Aristotle's *Organon* in the original Greek. Until at last, at the age of fifteen, this extraordinary intellect became homeless when his uneducated father discovered him perusing a philosophy treatise in Sanskrit—and expelled him from the family's house for being a black magic freak.

The next chapter of Pitts's life would inspire the 1997 Hollywood blockbuster romance *Good Will Hunting*. But it was anything but happy or glamorous for Pitts. He made his way to the University of Chicago, where in 1938, he covertly attended visiting lectures delivered by Bertrand Russell. Russell was startled to see the bereft teenager, but brokered a connection to the Viennese language-logician Rudolf Carnap, who found Pitts a job as a university janitor. Pitts gratefully accepted this faculty-proximate position, yet slowly, his mind turned inward. Becoming reclusive and paranoid, he started drinking heavily, precipitating, two short decades thence, death by esophageal bleeding.

While slipping down this tragic slope, however, Pitts enjoyed what seemed a stroke of luck: in 1942, at a Chicago colloquium, he collided with the recently arrived McCulloch. McCulloch was so struck by Pitts's unconventional intelligence that he promptly invited the nineteen-year-old to bunk at his rural homestead in Hinsdale, and there, after the McCulloch children were tucked into bed, the two unusual minds mingled their singular views, a mingling that, one year later, yielded a world-astonishing paper.

Titled "A Logical Calculus of the Ideas Imminent in Nervous Activity," the paper was published in the *Bulletin of Mathematical Biophysics*. It claimed that "neural events and the relations among them can be treated by means of propositional logic." Or in other words, that the human brain's hardwired operating system could be modeled by the AND-OR-NOT of Aristotle's *Organon*.

For readers not steeped in Pitts's know-how of Greek philosophy or McCulloch's numerological psychiatry, the implications of this statement took a few moments to process. But after those moments, the readers' eyebrows shot up in amazement. For if Pitts and McCulloch were right, then there followed two extraordinary consequences. The first was that Pitts and McCulloch had proved what Domarus had intuited: sane minds thought in pure symbolic logic. This meant that all the brain's healthy operations took the form of induction, deduction, interpretation, and other syllogistic processes. Which meant, in turn, that all the intelligent things that humans had done—in science, technology, art, business, politics, literature—could be reduced to AND-OR-NOT formulas. Out of those formulas had come the physics of Einstein, the plays of Shakespeare, the contraptions of Tesla, the paintings of van Gogh, the wealth of J. P. Morgan, the republic of the American Founding Fathers, and *everything, everything, everything* that the most brilliant of our species had created.

The second extraordinary consequence was that a machine could be built to think like those brilliant minds. Symbolic logic, after all, hewed to rules that could be embodied in an electronic-gate apparatus. That apparatus could then be programmed with formulas to cogitate like Einstein, Shakespeare, Tesla, and all the rest. And, even better, *the apparatus could compute improved formulas.* It could be fed Einstein's equations, Shakespeare's scripts, and Tesla's blueprints, and from that data, it could use its logical smarts to induct, deduct, and interpret its way to better and better—and finally, perfect—algorithms. At the flick of a digital switch, the world would be flooded with ultimate science, ultimate technology, ultimate government, ultimate culture, ultimate art. Utopia was logically imminent.

So mind-spinning was this vision that it seemed at first a reality break. The world had suffered a short circuit of logic, joining the Bonn schizophrenics in dream. But Pitts and McCulloch's paper was perfectly real, and it was soon to get realer. Because three years later, in 1946, the Einstein-Shakespeare-Tesla machine got built.

THE RATIONAL, SENSE-MAKING MACHINE

Pitts and McCulloch weren't the first to propose that human intelligence could be reduced to an automated symbolic-logic processor.

The proposal originated in Pitts's own master text, Aristotle's *Organon*, which posited a theory of human language in which words represented cognitive archetypes. According to that theory, our intelligent thoughts could be expressed in universal symbols that could in turn be processed by an automatic calculus, implying that human minds (or at least the minds of trained philosophers) were general logic engines.

This view of intelligence became the reigning dogma of the European Middle Ages, when *Organon*-reading friars (such as Thomas Aquinas) imagined God's psyche as an omniscient rational calculator. And after the collapse of medieval theology, it was reborn in Enlightenment philosophy:

- In 1655, Thomas Hobbes deduced in *De Corpore* that human intelligence was an addition-subtraction automaton: "by reasoning, I understand computation."
- In 1666, a twenty-year-old Gottfried Leibniz (as a twenty-year-old Pitts discovered to his fascination) penned *On the Combinatorial Art*, which theorized the existence of a mind

machine that could deploy a logical clockwork to crunch the symbolic language of human thought into the ultimate truth of everything.

■ In 1854, the rogue British logician George Boole argued in *The Laws of Thought* that human reason could be summed in algebraic equations that captured the rote action of Aristotle's syllogisms.

Yet even though McCulloch and Pitts's basic idea was not new, it was well timed. Seven years earlier, in 1936, the youthful mathematician Alan Turing had proved in a revolutionary paper: "It is possible to invent a single machine which can be used to compute any computable sequence." A year later, at an MIT lab, that theoretical machine was given a practical blueprint by the even more youthful Claude Shannon, who demonstrated in his master's thesis that electronic switches could automate Boole's algebraic equations. The result was the Arithmetic Logic Unit, or as we now know it, the computer.

The computer first appeared in downtown Philadelphia, a few blocks west of the Schuylkill River, and swiftly expanded into the 18,000 vacuum tubes, 6,000 switches, and 30-ton bulk of the Electronic Numerical Integrator and Computer, or ENIAC. ENIAC was designed in 1943, a few months before Pitts and McCulloch published their paper, and it whirred to life three years later. It deployed Shannon's blueprint and fulfilled Turing's conditions. It was, in other words, an automatic logician, powered by Boolean algebra and capable of solving all the problems that could be cracked by Aristotelian syllogisms.

In the end, ENIAC did not solve all—or indeed, very many—of those problems. It was mostly used to compute the physics of field artillery and hydrogen bombs. But its limited output did not discourage McCulloch and Pitts. They predicted that ENIAC would be upgraded, and true to their prediction, the eight decades since have brought remarkable improvements.

Those improvements fall into two broad categories: hardware and software. The hardware improvements (the biggest of which was the 1959 invention of the MOS transistor by Bell Lab scientists Dawon Kahng and Mohamed Atalla) allow for increased computing power, to the point that we now possess CPUs that can perform quadrillions of operations per second. The software improvements, meanwhile, have allowed for increased specialization and refinement:

- Thanks to the development of assembly language operating systems such as LINUX, computers can be adapted efficiently to a vast range of logical computation.
- Thanks to the development of Bayesian software, computers can cogitate in probabilities.
- Thanks to the development of machine-learning algorithms, computers can teach themselves faster than humans can program.

Taken as a whole, these upgrades have made computers quicker, more rangy, and more nuanced at logic. And that, in turn, has yielded two great results.

The first is the mainstreaming of Pitts and McCulloch's equation of human intelligence with automated symbolic logic. This mainstreaming can be seen across modern universities in the rise of computational theories of mind. Those theories were initially developed by philosophers such as Hilary Putnam and Jerry Fodor, and they've permeated the influential fields of cognitive science and evolutionary biology. So it is that a great many scholars who study the brain approach it as a logical apparatus that inducts through its eyes and ears, then deducts, infers, and interprets through "sense-making" neural networks.

Outside the academy, this way of thinking has become pervasive in broad swaths of the general public. It has made "logical" synonymous with "intelligent" in ordinary parlance. It has spawned hordes of self-help experts who, in diet books and TV finance shows, counsel us to look at the data, crunch the numbers, obey the statistics. It has birthed the corporate-educational phenomenon known as "design thinking." And it has produced the near ubiquity of business analytics: when picking stocks, building sports rosters, marketing, or doing anything else money related, expert analysts funnel big data and digitized spreadsheets into rational-choice theory (another logic product).

The second result is that, at long last, philosophy's confidence in logic can be put to the test. Previously, the test was doomed by a seemingly insuperable problem: humans. Humans were the philosopher-kings in charge of Plato's republic; humans were the theologians who interpreted God's biblical commandments; humans were the doctors who debugged the brains of shell-shocked schizophrenics. And humans are imperfect. Our neural operating system sputters with biological quirks, erratic emotions, and local data. To have us institute a more logical life is to have Rockland's inmates fix the asylum.

But now, our mortal shortcomings can be exorcised. Control of society can be handed entirely to logic. Logic can build an AI that never deviates from math and syllogisms.

Logic can invent a supercomputer that possesses McCulloch and Pitts's intelligence without succumbing to their fleshly frailties. Logic can combine modern engineering with medieval theology to design an Almighty to redeem us from ourselves.

Thus it is that Domarus's great experiment has launched. As you read these pages, billions of dollars are flowing across the globe into AI research. And billions more dollars of digital infrastructure are humming away, gathering data, crunching numbers, spitting out recommendations on how to run global economies, multinational corporations, health care systems, educational institutions, democratic governments, and the rest of our human intelligence network.

But already the experiment has failed.

73

THE FAILED EXPERIMENT

Computer AI fails at most human-thinking tasks. It can't create scientific hypotheses. It can't imagine novels. It can't invent technologies. It can't, that is, do anything that requires it to plan or process original actions.

This failure has prompted many different explanations from AI advocates: *AI just needs more processing power; AI just needs more contextual data; AI just needs upgraded software.* And even: *AI just needs to achieve consciousness.* But the simple truth is: AI's failure to human think is not correctable. The failure is forever.

There are many ways to prove this, but they can all be distilled to the fact that logic and story involve different physical mechanisms of intelligence, each with its own material limit. Story's limit is that it cannot ever yield eternal verities. Logic's limit is that it cannot ever process actions.

These limits are two sides of the same ontological coin:

- Story is a tool for sequencing, combining, and generating actions; actions are temporal; the temporal is not timeless; and the not timeless cannot be forever true.
- Logic, in contrast, *can* be forever true. That's because logic is a tool for computing numbers, representations, and other symbols. And symbols are timeless. They exist, unchanging, in the eternal present tense of logic's "X is Y" and math's "1 + 1 is 2."

Because logic can do what story can't, it can't do what story can: process actions. Actions include, at minimum, a cause and its effect, and those two elements cannot exist concurrently in logic's eternal *is*. A cause must precede its effect in time, necessitating either a past or a future. Which means that when actions are fed into a logical system, the system is confronted with an insoluble problem: *Render a cause and its effect into a single, present-tense instant.* Or in other words: *Take two things that can't coexist—and make them simultaneous.*

This logic buster has been acknowledged by logicians as far back as Aristotle. Aristotle observes in *Organon* that logic can process actions only by rendering them into qualities. (E.g., the action *to reason* must be rendered into the quality *rational,* turning the narrative "Aristotle reasons" into the subject-predicate proposition "Aristotle is rational.") Since qualities are unchanging, the effect of this rendering is to deactivate action, discarding its essence: motion. In other words: to save logic from being broken by action, action is ghosted from the *Organon's* logical system.

The same evaporation of action remains the sole way that the logic gates of modern AI can handle the narrative operations processed automatically by human brains, as we can see from the procedure that computerized Natural Language Processors (NLPs) use to translate our everyday speech into binary machine code. The procedure converts action verbs (e.g., *Jane runs*) into linking verbs and participles (e.g., *Jane is running*). The double upshot is (1) to equate the action's cause (*Jane*) with its effect (*running*); and (2) to make the action (*runs*) a timeless state (*running*) with no beginning, effectively deleting the action's origin.

Neither upshot is significant within logic's timeless domain of correlation, but when we exit logic for the temporal world of causation, both have eerily unnatural consequences. The consequence of (1), that is, of equating causes with their effects, is to make action symbolic, precipitating magical thinking. The consequence of (2), that is, of severing effects from their causes, is to rob causes of their physical function, making them causes in name only.

Together, these consequences replace mechanics with semiotics, substituting signification for action. Symbols are mystically transubstantiated into causes while material actors are divested of their mechanical nature, luring us into believing that magic incantations, words of power, and priestly rituals can change reality—and that gravity, fire, and other physical forces are made of the same ontological stuff as alphabet letters, ASCII characters, and mathematical formulas.

This logical distortion of physics is what happened in medieval science. Powered by Aristotle's *Organon*, the

European natural philosophers of the late Middle Ages reduced material actors to verbiage (final cause, formal cause, efficient cause) and embraced language as a causal agent: "In the beginning was the Word." Nature became a web of symbols and life an allegory.

The same thing happened in twentieth-century literature departments (see chapter 4) when character criticism was replaced by semiotics: language became power and representation, reality. And the same thing is happening now in computer AI. Which is why computer AI—no less than fourteenth-century science and twentieth-century literary criticism—runs afoul of earthly physics. And which is also why computer AI will never do what Domarus, McCulloch, and Pitts dreamed: obsolesce human intelligence. Human intelligence can fathom the distinction between a cause and its effect, so while computers are stuck permanently in a semiotic zone of magic, we humans can operate as scientists, grasping the forces of nature and leveraging them into original creations.

How do we humans have this capacity to think in cause and effect? Is it because our brain possesses consciousness, intuition, or some other fuzzily "emergent" property? No. As we will explore in the following chapter, our brain is as reductively mechanical in its operations as computer transistors. It simply possesses different machinery.

Narrative machinery.

6

The Brain Machinery of Storythinking

It was the summer of 1951 at a little brick lab in southern New Zealand. And as evening dropped in pink and gold, a bespectacled scientist with trim gray hair and a trim white coat unlocked a metal cage, selecting a frightened cat to shave.

The scientist was John Eccles. In his lab, he had shaved many a cat. But this cat would be different. It would provide Eccles with a peek at the brain's plugs and cables, earning him a Nobel Prize and revealing the machinery of storythinking.

That machinery, as Eccles saw, has two main components: (1) self-powered electronic wires and (2) nonelectronic connectors.

The self-powered electronic wires are neurons, the biological marvel we explored in chapter 3. Their electronics allow them to think fast, fast, fast. And their self-powering enables them to initiate action: *do this.*

The nonelectronic connectors are synapses, the biological marvel that Eccles was probing at his New Zealand lab. Synapses can link one action to another. And because they're nonelectronic, they can operate free from the constraints of design, improvising narrative scripts beyond the laws of logic.

Neurons and synapses are wildly unlike the machinery found in computers. That computer machinery can be built of electric switches, vacuum tubes, or silicon transistors, but it all amounts to mechanisms for running (1) binary and (2) NAND/NOR logic gates. Or, as formally articulated in 1965 by Alan Turing's protégé I. J. Good: (1) a symbolic language and (2) a set of fixed rules.

How do these two computer components relate to the two components of storythinking? Well, "a symbolic language" is so different from "self-powered wires" and "a set of fixed rules" so different from "nonelectronic connectors" that to compare them risks distorting more than it clarifies. But as a rough distinction, we could say that our storythinking brain can rewire its hardware, while the computer can only rewrite its software. And although computer software can do a great deal, it must do it all through the computer CPU's three hardwired actions: AND, OR, NOT. Which means that while our brain can devise original actions, the computer is always running combinations of the same fixed logic operations.

The functional cash-out of these mechanical differences is that computers can pick the best available option—while our brain can imagine new options. Or, more briskly, that computers are deciders while our brain is an innovator. For evidence-based judgment, you want a computer. For creative action, thank your neurons and their synapses.

This isn't to say that computers can't be creative; they can. But it is to say that their creativity extends only to the semiotic, and the semiotic (as we saw in chapter 5) does not contain action. To a computer, being creative is randomly mix-and-matching words, images, and other timeless symbols from divergent sets. To the human brain, being creative is guessing a new cause, then testing its effect. Which is why computer AI can engineer new haikus and pixel faces but will never invent strategies, novels, scientific hypotheses, or anything else requiring narrative.

This mechanical distinction between computers and brains has been repeatedly fudged by AI purveyors in the seven decades since Eccles's 1951 experiment. But the distinction is important to enforce—not to denigrate computers or to preserve human ineffability, but because it is crucial for understanding how to upgrade our own mental performance. That upgrade won't happen if we persist in downplaying the differences between animal neurons and silicon transistors. Instead, we'll keep cranking out counterproductive educational curricula like the Common Core (see chapter 4). To do better, we need to grasp what's distinct about our head technology, so that rather than trying to force-program it to perform critical thinking, data-driven decision making, and other computational tasks, we craft pedagogical rubrics tailored to our brain's storythinking strengths: creativity, adaptability, growth.

One such rubric will be outlined in chapter 7, which will describe a few processes you can run on your gray matter to boost storythinking. But to provide a hardware foundation for those software enhancements, this chapter will explore the backstory of Eccles's cat experiment, touring a historical collection of characters who include a tortured twentieth-century logician, a Renaissance revolutionary who almost launched modern science, and a Victorian astronomer who actually did.

From those characters, we'll learn about the nonlogical neural machinery that Eccles glimpsed. And as we stretch our brain to connect their biographies into a single narrative, we'll experience that machinery ourselves.

OUR STORY'S FIRST CHARACTERS: ECCLES AND THE SOUPS

Eccles had never heard (and never would hear) of storythinking, so he had no idea that he was on the verge of advancing its study. Yet as he shaved the cat on that midcentury eve, he did know that he was about to run a highly illuminating experiment.

The experiment was the culmination of a long struggle that dated back to modern science's origins in the seventeenth century. But its immediate purpose was to resolve a more recent fight. That fight had started with a point of agreement: the neuroscientists of the 1940s all concurred that the neuron was electric. It fired a charge—the action potential—down a winding axon stalk via a battery of salt-ion channels into the neuron's terminal, where a tiny gap—the synapse—separated the charge from another brain cell.

Here, however, a question arose: How did the charge hop the gap, sparking the neighboring cell? Two answers were proposed, one by a group of scientists who styled themselves "sparks" and the other by a group who styled themselves "soups."

The sparks thought: the charge itself hopped the gap, zapping like a lightning bolt across the synapse. After all, if the neuron was electric, then surely the junction was too. That would make the entire brain electronic, reducing all thought to voltage whizzing through circuits. This was the simplest—and most elegant—model of human intelligence. Which is to say: it was the most *logical* model, because logic dictated parsimony.

Yet despite such sophisticated arguments from logic, the soups had an opposing answer: the synapse was non-electronic. It was traversed not by electrical brainwaves but by chemicals dumped into the gap. Was the dumping simple or elegant? No, it was not, the soups conceded. But they had run many clever experiments that suggested it was nevertheless how neurons worked.

This soupy contention had been relayed to John Eccles in the late 1920s when he was a Rhodes Scholar at Magdalen College, Oxford. Immediately, it had struck him as ludicrous. How could chemicals float at the velocity of thought? And why would neurons have evolved such a convoluted mechanism for communicating with one another? Why wouldn't they have stuck with the fast-acting electrical system they already had?

Convinced by this rational deduction, Eccles set out to confirm it with empiricism. Throughout the 1930s, as he made his way from Oxford to Australia, he ran a series of ingenious experiments on frog and feline neuromuscular junctions. Those experiments revealed that synaptic transmission was fast—so fast that it was inconceivable to Eccles that it could be occurring at anything less than electricity's lightspeed.

The soups, however, remained unmoved. They stuck doggedly to their hypothesis of chemical transmission, enraging Eccles and impelling him to act. In May 1935 he publicly derided the soups at the annual meeting of the Physiology Society. This "very tense encounter" precipitated a pointed exchange of letters between Eccles and the soups' smugly placid leader, Nobel laureate Henry Dale. And over the following years, their scientific disagreement escalated into "war."

The war raged through the 1940s, as the world itself convulsed in violence. And long after a global armistice was signed in 1945, the sparks and soups battled on. Until at last, in the early 1950s, Eccles struck upon a brilliant strategy for concluding the struggle.

Eccles had by then relocated from Australia to New Zealand, where he'd met an awkwardly earnest Austrian scholar who'd fled the Nazis to take up a philosophy lectureship at Canterbury University College. A scholar with a creatively idiosyncratic take on the working of science.

A scholar named Karl Popper.

CHARACTER THREE: THE TORTURED LOGICIAN KARL POPPER

Karl Popper would, in the dusk of his career, come to be regarded as one of the twentieth century's most influentially original thinkers. But at the time he met Eccles, he was viewed as a minor curiosity, his mind at strenuous odds with contemporary philosophy—and indeed, with its own psychology.

The conflict in Popper's psyche sprang from his dual intellectual nature. On the one hand, he was gripped from childhood by a love for logic, a love so pure that it could not tolerate the slightest deviation from absolute reason. On the other hand, he was entranced by the material world and its living things: humans, cultures, markets. And because these living things, by virtue of their dynamism in time, defied the static eternities of logical equation, Popper was forever shattering one of his loves with the other. He would embrace logic—and tear it apart with life. He would embrace life—and tear it apart with logic.

This state of exquisite inner tension made Popper's existence an agony of reluctant iconoclasm. Time and again, he arrived at a temple of learning, hopeful of joining its reverent congregation—only to instead smash the altar, exposing idolatry.

The smashing began when Popper debunked his teenage idol, Karl Marx. Marx had wielded Hegel's dialectic (see chapter 8) to construct what he viewed as an unassailably rational theory of economic history. But Popper relentlessly detected the theory's failed predictions: *contra* Marx, the middle class had not disappeared; *contra* Marx, there had not been a death spiral of overproduction; *contra* Marx, the capitalists had not been everywhere overthrown by a chain reaction of proletarian revolutions. And with a cry of horror at his own apostasy, Popper pulled Marx's mighty structure down.

Next, Popper turned on Sigmund Freud. Freud had been more cursory in his reasoning than Marx but also more canny, basing his theories of human psychology in tautologies that twisted objections into proofs. Yet Popper was not intimidated by Freud's ingenious labyrinth. Plunging unflinchingly into its circular logic, he grabbed its murky sophistries and dragged them out into the sun, revealing psychoanalysis as a beguiling con.

It was in this idol-breaking frame of mind that Popper arrived in the 1920s at Vienna's recently established Pädagogisches Institut—Pedagogical Institute. Enrolling to pursue a psychology doctorate, the twenty-something Popper set his uncompromising gaze on modern science. And as he inspected the grand theories of recent physicists, he found himself drawn into a tussle that dated back three centuries to the 1620 *Novum Organum*—that is, New Logic—of Francis Bacon.

CHARACTER FOUR: FRANCIS BACON, THE ALMOST-FOUNDER OF MODERN SCIENCE

Bacon was, like Popper, an iconoclast, albeit a less reluctant one.

Castigating the European universities of his day for anchoring nature's study in deduction, which worked top down to impose preexisting ideologies on subsequent discoveries, he called for a pivot to deduction's opposite: induction. Induction used data to update existing rules, so Bacon believed that it would inject vitality into the study of physics. Fresh facts would be gathered through an energetic program of observation and experiment, powered by astral telescopes and atomic microscopes. And instead of being deducted into old theories, those facts would be *inducted* into *new* theories, lifting science out of medieval stasis into modern progress.

This shift toward induction was hailed by Bacon's fellow Englishmen—most famously Isaac Newton—as the beginning of a revolution. But in point of fact, the revolution was only partly revolutionary. Induction was, after all, one of the traditional logical processes championed in Aristotle's *Organon*, the textbook foundation of epistemology in the Middle Ages. So, by championing an inductive method,

Bacon was not distancing himself as radically from medieval science as his insurgent rhetoric implied.

Thus it was that Bacon continued the Aristotelian schoolmen's practice of treating the physical world as a text: the "book of nature." Thus it was that Bacon's acolytes maintained the old practice of referring to physicists as philosophers of nature, or more succinctly, natural philosophers. And thus it was that Bacon's new philosophers retained the medieval practice of treating knowledge as strictly logical: symbolic data was inserted into science's inductive machine, which, like the syllogisms of the Middle Ages, automatically computed the mathematical laws of nature.

This quasi-new, quasi-traditional, Baconian-Aristotelian logic processor hummed along, unchallenged in England, through Newton and the eighteenth century. Yet against what Bacon had predicted, the processor did not yield enlightened consensus. Instead, natural philosophy was riven by endless disputes, because even when everyone agreed upon a basic fact, they quarreled over how to interpret it. The same data that prompted one natural philosopher to conclude that light was a corpuscle prompted another to conclude that it was instead a longitudinal vibration. The same data that prompted one natural philosopher to posit that gravity was action at a distance prompted another to argue for the existence of invisible astral fluids.

That such bickering was the result of applying logic to "the book" of nature should not have been a surprise, for logic had malfunctioned in identical fashion when applied to another weighty tome: the Bible. Rather than building gradually but inexorably toward unanimity, logic had assiduously inducted the Bible's historical, linguistic, and symbolic data—then churned out the competing doctrines of Catholicism, Calvinism, Unitarianism, and other Christian sects.

And indeed, this tendency of induction to proliferate interpretations is why Europe's feudal universities had all along preferred deduction. The university faculty did not disagree with Bacon's fundamental point: deduction was a retardant of intellectual progress. Yet to them, there was value in the retardant, not least because by maintaining the old theories, it also maintained cohesion and stability. And were not cohesion and stability two necessary features of any logical system? And had these features not been disarrayed by Bacon's so-called reform, riddling his "new logic" with flux and fragmentation?

Hence early nineteenth-century physics found itself in crisis. Instead of achieving exultant unanimity, it had been sucked into the same infighting that had sundered the theology of the Middle Ages. Clearly, if moderns were to outdo medievals, science would have to undergo a more profound methodological revolution, one that carried it beyond Bacon.

And science did undergo that second revolution. Because in 1830, a jump forward was made by another iconoclast: the royal astronomer John Herschel.

CHARACTER FIVE: JOHN HERSCHEL AND THE MODERN SCIENTIFIC METHOD

John Herschel was as gorgeously-tragically divided of mind as Popper.

Born with a butterfly intelligence, Herschel flitted between scholarly flowers: chemistry, poetry, mathematics, minerology, physics, painting, photography. But wherever he winged, he could not escape the long shadow of his father, William, an astronomer of such global celebrity that he'd hobnobbed with the English king, the German royal family, and pre-Waterloo Napoleon.

Stricken by a filial sense of obligation to reach an equal zenith of achievement, young John procured his own telescope and chained himself to its eyepiece each twilight, determined to map every glowing object in the sky. This epic task required so much discipline that it turned young John machine. Ruthlessly restraining his nomadic curiosity, he cranked through automatic midnight after automatic midnight, surveying the sable constellations with such inflexible precision that he logged coordinates (checked in triplicate) for more than 70,000 stars. Until his dazzling persistence was rewarded with the Royal Society's Copley Medal for outstanding scientific research, not once but twice, trumping the medal count of his one-time-winning father.

Yet even though John Herschel outdid his father by being an inductive engine, his most enduring contribution to science came from releasing (at last) his butterfly brain. The release came in the late 1820s as Herschel was composing a popular introduction to science, *A Preliminary Discourse on the Study of Natural History*. The work's monotonous title reflected its author's iron resolve to be a responsible scientist, but tucked into its pages was a wild departure from scientific norms. For as Herschel attempted to explain the scientific method to his lay audience, he crashed against the problem that induction simply didn't work. And rather than dutifully recycling Bacon's malfunctioning logic, he bravely conjured up a new hypothesis: *Instead of distilling millions of inductions into logical law, the scientist's mind jumps from a few data points to hypothesize a provisional cause, which it uses to narrate bold predictions that can be verified via experiment.*

Or in Herschel's words: "Such is the tendency of the human mind to speculation, that on the least idea of an analogy between a few phenomena, it leaps forward, as it were, to a cause or law, to the temporary neglect of all the rest; so that, in fact, almost all our principal inductions must be regarded as a series of ascents and descents, and of conclusions from a few cases, verified by trial on many." Such "leap[ing]" to a possible "cause," Herschel pointed out, was how Nicolas Copernicus had overturned the medieval view of the solar system. The solar system had not been inducted in every minute detail, yet Copernicus had seen enough through his telescopic lenses to identify a flaw in the traditional theory that the earth sat, still, at the system's center. So, off the facts that he possessed, Copernicus vaulted to a new narrative: *the earth orbited the sun.* That narrative then yielded the astonishing prediction that the planet Venus had crescent phases—a prediction that subsequent astronomers confirmed.

With this reformulation of the Copernican Revolution, Herschel provoked high alarm in England's scientific establishment. Herschel's good friend William Whewell—a forward-enough thinker to have coined the term "scientist" as a replacement for "natural philosopher"—agitatedly responded that Herschel's method of speculative leaps would mean that science wasn't really science; it was a "guess." To fend off this incursion of imagination into the scientific method, Whewell sternly reminded his friend about Bacon's warning against vaulting past the facts— and about Herschel's own celebration of Newton. Had Newton not been utterly opposed to notional guesswork?

Had Newton not, when pressed for an explanation for gravity, famously replied, "Hypotheses non fingo"—"I don't jump to conclusions"? Had Newton not stuck always to inductive mathematics?

Herschel persisted, however, in his incautious apostasy, for his years of patient induction had revealed to him that both the Old (medieval) Logic and the New (Baconian) Logic were wrong. During his nocturnal vigils, he had collected more raw data than Aristotle or Newton—or indeed, anyone else in history. Yet that raw data had not produced any major scientific breakthroughs. Such breakthroughs, he saw now, required narrative conjectures. That was how science really advanced.

True to Herschel's own conjecture, this was how nineteenth-century science itself proceeded. Shortly after Herschel's book was published in 1830, it was read avidly by a young Charles Darwin, who leveraged its conjecture-then-test method to leap from a few Galapagos finches to the hypothesis of evolution by natural selection. After which, Darwin devoted himself to confirming his speculation via predictions about the particulars of blue-eyed cats, dung beetles, and human emotions.

In 1871, Herschel was buried at Westminster Abbey, where his grave now sits between the tombs of Newton and Darwin, a fitting place for the man who served as the transition between the Enlightenment scientific method of computational induction and the modern scientific method of narrative speculation. But even though Herschel had made room in science for creative experiment, logic's ghost still lingered.

Until six decades after Herschel was laid to rest, a final exorcism was performed by Karl Popper.

89

FROM HERSCHEL BACK TO POPPER

Popper was drawn into science by the work of Albert Einstein.

(Einstein is this chapter's seventh protagonist, after Eccles, the soups, Popper, Bacon, Herschel, and Darwin. Which means that you might be feeling a bit lost in all the characters and their subplots. *What do these people have to do with storythinking? Or even with each other?*

If such questions are creeping into your head, here are two ways to answer them:

1. Rewind the previous pages to focus on the narrative jumps from character to character, helping your synapses do a Copernicus (see the previous section) and hypothesize *why*.
2. Keep forging ahead in half-comprehension until you reach the chapter's end, enabling your synapses to do like the character critics (see chapter 4) and reverse-engineer the overall plot via causal thinking.

Why should you bother doing that extra work when this chapter's author could have spared you the trouble by trimming a few characters? Because the instant you grasp *why* the soup-spark war leads to Herschel's telescope leads to Albert Einstein, you'll feel your synapses connect a vast range of actors into a single sequence of events, confirming the power of your brain's storythinking machinery by experiencing it, firsthand.)

Einstein, like Darwin, made a narrative leap. After spotting a few anomalies in science's existing theories, he used a sequence of storythinking imaginations—where he ran alongside sunbeams and dreamed of "a beam of light as an electromagnetic field at rest though spatially oscillating"—to invent a new theory, relativity, in which gravity bent light to a different degree than in Newton's old physics.

Einstein's adventurous prediction was put to the test in 1919, when the British astronomers Arthur Stanley Eddington and Frank Watson Dyson journeyed to West Africa and East Brazil with giant lenses for photographing the May 29 solar eclipse. Six months later, the snapshot results were announced to a dumbfounded world: Einstein had predicted right! Relativity was true!

Popper was enthralled—yet skeptical. Typically split of mind, he was convinced that Einstein's theory differed from the pseudoscience of Marx and Freud—yet simultaneously convinced that it was logically incomplete. And as Popper bent his ferocious reason to scrutinize the data before him, he realized: both sides of his mind were right. Einstein's theory wasn't pseudoscience, and it also wasn't a logical proof. Against what the world believed, relativity had *not* been verified by the 1919 solar eclipse. This was because verification exceeded the power of empirical experiments: experiments couldn't confirm a scientific theory, any more than an anecdote (or indeed, a billion anecdotes) could confirm an absolute truth. Yet even so, Popper saw that Einstein had gone beyond Marx and Freud. His new theory of light had operated as a counter-narrative that had successfully anticipated the major plot twist of the Eddington-Dyson expedition. And now that the twist had transpired, Einstein's theory could be used to predict further plot twists that could themselves be tested via innovative experiments, creatively expanding the practice of science.

With this, Popper proved what Herschel had intuited: science wasn't built of logic. It was built of speculative narratives from outlying events. To the extent that logic played a role, it was to debunk errant hypotheses and establish the permanent uncertainty of the remainder, encouraging inventive research like Eddington and Dyson's globetrotting supercameras.

In 1934, Popper sketched the basics of this scientific method in *Logik der Forschung*—*The Logic of Scientific Discovery*—a tersely worded monograph that produced a mix of apathy and head scratching. For as readers slowly unriddled Popper's dense prose, they realized that his title was misleading: the work it designated was not so much a logic as an unlogic. Rather than providing a systematic calculus for doing science, it urged scientists to be as imaginative as Einstein—and to then dedicate themselves to falsifying what they'd just imagined.

Befuddled as to how they were to achieve such great flights of fancy (and equally befuddled as to why they would then want to turn against their own creations), the book's readers therefore acted rationally: they ignored Popper's method and kept up their bickering over different interpretations of the same inductions.

Hence it was that Popper found himself relegated to his anonymous faculty position in New Zealand. But when Popper met Eccles, Eccles realized: Popper's method could help end the soup-spark disagreement. In the past, both sides had devoted their energies to proving they were right. Yet now, following Popper's method, Eccles would do the opposite: run an experiment to prove he was wrong. If the experiment failed, he'd then set about debunking the soups. If the experiment succeeded, he'd concede that there was more to the brain than electricity.

So, that's what Eccles did on the warm summer's eve in 1951. He sedated the frightened cat and shaved its lower back. He prepared an intracellular electrode, its tip so narrow that it could plug into a single feline nerve. He slid the electrode into the sleeping animal's spinal cord, tapping a quadriceps motor neuron. And he fixed his eyes on a cathode-ray amplifier, a blinking technology that measured the neuron's transmembrane voltage. If the voltage fell, that would instantly falsify the spark hypothesis, proving that Eccles had, for his entire career, been wrong.

The voltage plunged. *Eccles had been totally, utterly mistaken.* His electronic theory of the synapse evaporated in a cathode blink. But while the experiment falsified Eccles's prior publications, it affirmed something else: his worth as a scientist. Instantly acknowledging that he'd been incorrect, he dashed off a letter to his rival Henry Dale, conceding defeat. The war with the soups had ended. The sparks were extinguished.

Dale was extremely pleased. He wrote Eccles back, congratulating his "newfound enthusiasm" for the soups' position. But Dale's self-satisfaction led him astray. Eccles hadn't become a soup. Instead, hewing strictly to Popper's method, he'd just stopped being a spark. He'd come to acknowledge that there was more to the brain than electricity—a more that might conform to the soup synapse but also might ramble elsewhere, into the unknown.

Subsequent experiments have confirmed this latter possibility. Where the soups focused their attention on a single chemical neurotransmitter (acetylcholine), we now think that the synapse contains an enormous variety of machinery, some of it chemical, much of it peptide. Are we right about that? We can never say for sure. But thanks to Eccles—who'd be granted his own Nobel in 1963 for his summer eve experiment—we can be quite certain that the brain is more than electric.

Which, to pull together this chapter's wending historical narrative, explains how the brain can do the Herschel-Popper method of science, escaping the strictures of logical induction to speculate creatively.

THE BRAIN MACHINERY OF SCIENTIFIC SPECULATION

The more-than-electric brain machinery glimpsed by Eccles emerged about a billion years ago in tentacle-mouthed jellyfish known as archaic cnidarians.

Those cnidarians possessed special cells that paralyzed prey with stinging peptides . . . until through an act of happenstance, the peptides were repurposed as internal stingers. Instead of being dumped into external ocean waters, they were deployed by one cnidarian cell to jolt another into acting.

This peptide system was the genesis of the animal synapse. (Or at least, that's our best unfalsified guess.) And as the cnidarian peptide cells specialized, becoming neurons, the synapse revealed an unexpected potential: it could do more than link neurons to other kinds of cells. It could link *neurons to neurons*, such that one action activated another, activated another, activated another.

Thus started the animal nervous system, leading eventually to the feline spine—and the human brain.

The human brain contains a vast number of neurons. (Our current best guess is about 85 billion.) And most of those neurons are synaptically interconnected. They're part of a hugely involuted jellyfish that is incessantly stinging itself.

Why? Why so many neurons, jolting each other with peptides? Why has the synapse's machinery become such a gigantic part of our headspace?

The answer from logic is: *storage and processing power.* But if that's what our synapses are providing, they're extraordinarily bad at their job. Our brain's memory is weak—and dodgy. It can record far less raw information than a comparatively sized hard drive and recall it with much less accuracy. Nor is our brain that good at crunching data. If it were, then we wouldn't need to spend so many agonizing years in school, grinding away at math and critical thinking.

The alternative hypothesis from storythinking is that our synapses are contributing to the brain's core behavioral function: plotting original actions. How, exactly, synapses do that, we can't say. Yet we can, like Herschel and Darwin and Einstein, productively conjecture:

- Since our neurons contribute to plotting via the generation of actions . . .
- And since our synapses link one neuron to another . . .
- Our synapses contribute to plotting via the *linking* of actions.

Our synapses, that is, chain together individual actions into causal sequences, allowing our brain to improvise,

95

test, and revise cognitive narratives. By doing so, our synapses enlarge our neurons' trial-and-error process into an experimental method for inventing and adapting plans. On a micro level, the method works by speculatively generating (or eliminating) a *this-leads-to-that* connection between one neuron and another. On a macro level, it works by expanding, editing, branching, innovating, pruning, and redirecting our mental strategies.

This storythinking process is lent enormous plasticity by the sheer number of synapses in the human neocortex. They're estimated to be in the trillions, enabling our brain to fork and flex action scripts in almost endless new directions, innovating art, technology, business, and politics.

Such innovation lies beyond the power of computer AI. AI can only reiterate symbolic logic's three preprogrammed actions: AND, OR, NOT. Which is why AI is limited to deducing—based on the data flowing into it—what sport, science, or dance *is*. It cannot freestyle fresh actions that expand what sport, science, and dance *can do*.

To change this situation, we'd need to create a computer capable of rearranging its core architecture. Which is to say, we'd need to exchange the etched transistors of modern CPUs with free-floating hardware that could riff itself into original circuitry. Beyond the obvious engineering challenges that this poses, it's rendered impossible from the get-go by the fact that electronic systems are governed by mathematical equations of voltage and current. Step outside those equations, and the systems melt or shut down. This means that computer brains cannot be blindly improvised; they must be designed in advance to stick to the math. Such sticking is what their current logic gates are engineered, precisely, to do. But if those gates were freed to shuffle about, they'd swiftly unglue, frying themselves or blinking out.

For a thinking machine to get around this hurdle, it would thus have to be mechanically different from a computer. Instead of running a continuous electron flow from an outside power source, it would need its individual cables to be powered internally. And it would also need its cables to be buffered from one another, so that rather than passing on their electric charges like transistors do, they plug into one another nonelectrically, enabling them to ad lib action circuits that escape the design requirement of electronics.

Which, as Eccles discovered on that summer's eve, is exactly how the brain works.

97

THE BRAIN'S STORYTHINKING ARCHITECTURE

The brain is composed of neurons, which are electric cables powered internally (via mitochondrial ATP) and joined by nonelectric plugs (i.e., synapses).

This mixed architecture gives our neurons the benefit of both electronic and nonelectronic transmission. The benefit of the former is speed, empowering our thoughts to zip with light's rapidity. The benefit of the latter is experimental action; by enabling our neurons to freely alter their connections to each other, our synapses allow us to improvise our mental architecture in ways that purely electronic machines cannot. Thus it is that our gray matter can do what Darwin and Einstein did: hypothesize, imagine, think new. And thus it is that our species can speculate adaptively, giving us an edge in life's ever-shifting battle.

That battle—like every asymmetric conflict—is characterized by the two factors that John Herschel's Prussian contemporary Carl von Clausewitz detected in war: dynamic opposition that changes in response to our success, forcing us to counter-change; and an uncertain environment where evolving conditions produce intractable data "fog."

These factors are the demise of computer AI; its statistical methods cannot gain traction in volatility or murk. But both can be productively engaged by our neuroanatomy. Our neuroanatomy can operate with limited data, because limited data (as we saw in chapter 4) is the province of narrative, and narrative (as we've experienced in this chapter) is the province of our brain's synaptic machinery. Thanks to that machinery, we're able to survive in fast-changing, contested domains where the only intel is anomalous—and where we must constantly compete against original adversaries.

If we wanted to do an Eilhard von Domarus (see chapter 5) and devise an Artificial Intelligence that could out-strategize the human brain, we'd therefore need to pursue one of two routes: program a logical AI with all the facts of nature or invent a postcomputer AI that swaps out transistors for a mixed electronic-nonelectronic unit akin to the animal neuron. The first route lies beyond current science; the second, beyond current engineering.

Yet even though such superhuman AI lies past time's horizon, we'll see in the next chapter that we can still create a superior new intelligence. That intelligence is: us, with a story-software upgrade.

7

Improving Storythinking

In the spring of 1927, as red tulips popped in New York's city parks, the scholars of Columbia University's literature department peered closely at the wizard.

He had athletic legs and dark, wavy hair. And more enchantingly still, he possessed a mind that thought in fairy tales and legends.

With that mind, the wizard had discovered that his dreams contained a story. A story created by the author of the world's religions. A story that held the key to fathoming life's true meaning.

Yet even so, the wizard grasped less light than shadow: How exactly did the story start? Where precisely did it end? What middle chapters bound its cosmic plot?

Hungry to find out, the wizard made a request of Columbia's scholars: *Let me study the fables gathered on your bookshelves. Help me master their wide geographies and vast time scales, discovering the myth that connects the globe's great narratives into one.*

The scholars pondered this earnest proposal. And they decided: for all the wizard's charming seriousness, he was a wannabe. So, they denied him his PhD and forced him out of their department's new white halls to wander crumbling archives to the East, studying Sanskrit and troubadours. They condescended after his return, goading him to flee upstate to Woodstock, where he self-educated for five years in a rented shack filled with haphazardly gathered paperbacks. They smirked at his intellectual quest, calling it magic, mysticism, and theosophy.

But the wizard would laugh last. His quest led to a bestselling book and then the biggest blockbuster in Hollywood history. Until finally, he came back from the dead to whisper his gospel. A gospel that became—and remains—the world's most popular theory of story.

The wizard's name was Joseph Campbell. His bestseller was *The Hero with a Thousand Faces,* published in 1949 by Pantheon. His blockbuster was *Star Wars,* directed in 1977 by George Lucas. His posthumous gospel was *The Power of Myth,* aired in June 1988 on PBS with Bill Moyers.

From him, millions have taken a map to the ultimate story, a map known as the Hero's Journey. And even now, when so much has been gleaned from Campbell, we have more to learn. Because we always learn the most from mistakes. And the wizard made an epic error.

THE WIZARD'S ERROR

The scholars thought that Joseph Campbell's error was to foray into pseudoscience. First, he trusted in the monomyth.

Second, in the symbolism of dreams. Third, in a collective unconscious.

The first bit of pseudoscience came from James George Frazer's *The Golden Bough* (1890), which alleged that every global myth—from Africa to Asia to the Americas—was a rendition of the same eternal tale: a hero who sacrificed himself to resurrect the world. The second bit of pseudoscience came from Sigmund Freud's *The Interpretation of Dreams* (1899), which claimed that our nightly imaginations contained a symbolic language that could be decoded to reveal the repressed wishes of our unconscious. The third bit of pseudoscience came from Carl Jung's *Über die archetypen des kollektiven unbewussten* (1934), which, by merging Frazer and Freud with strains of Plato's philosophical idealism, styled our minds as buddings of an intergalactic psyche implanted with eternal archetypes: the hero, the mother, the teacher. Mashed together, these three pseudoscientific influences produced Campbell's theory of the Hero's Journey: *A universal human narrative that chronicles the metaphorical death and rebirth of our questing soul as it travels, like an ancient demigod into the underworld, to bring back life's sacred truth from the cavern of our shared unconscious.*

But although the scholars were right to brand this as magical thinking, that's not the real flaw in Campbell's approach to story. The real flaw is more fundamental. You can detect it in the very opening sentence of Campbell's 1949 bestseller: "Whether we listen with aloof amusement to the dreamlike mumbo jumbo of some red-eyed witch doctor of the Congo, or read with cultivated rapture thin translations from the sonnets of the mystic Lao-tse; now and again crack the hard nutshell of an argument of Aquinas, or catch suddenly the shining meaning of a bizarre Eskimo fairy tale: it will be always the one, shape-shifting yet marvelously constant story." At the bottom of this stream of outdated anthropology lies: "always the one . . . constant story." And that is the slip in Campbell's thinking. To seek one eternal story is to convert narrative into logic, like Aristotle did in *Topics* (see chapter 2). It's to think in terms of ideal *product* instead of practical *process*, chasing the metaphysical dream of ultimate truth at the expense of story's biological function: creative action.

To pinpoint this as Campbell's core mistake is to realize that it extends far beyond him. Plenty of academics who dismiss the Hero's Journey as quackery are guilty of treating story as a product, not a process. This is the error of modern philosophers, semioticians, screenwriting gurus, and AI researchers who try to reduce movies and novels to timeless story structures, fixed literary genres, or universal themes. This is the misstep made by anyone who believes that every successful Hollywood script or fiction paperback derives its plot from a shortlist of immortal formulas.

In order to escape this evolutionary dead end, we need to overturn Campbell's method. Instead of searching for the best narrative product, we need to search for *a better narrative process*. We need, that is, to find a more effective method for generating narrative plans and strategies that can help us navigate life's infinite possibilities.

That's the scientific answer to Campbell's quest. That's the real path to becoming a story wizard.

BECOMING A STORY WIZARD

Storythinking, as we've seen over the preceding chapters, is a neural refinement of Darwinian evolution. It's a more fruitful version of nature's blind mechanism of problem solving and innovation. If we want to storythink more expertly, we therefore need to continue refining evolution's core process. Or to be precise, we need to continue refining evolution's *two* core processes, creation and selection. Creation generates functional variety. Selection winnows that variety.

"Functional variety" is another way of saying: a diversity of causes. Causes are processes, so they're different from words, representations, and the other symbol stuff that Campbell saw as story's essence. That symbol stuff yields truth and its final products: morality and meaning. Causes, in contrast, yield action and its fluid offspring: change and opportunity.

Philosophically, all causes fall into the same ontological family. Practically, they vary widely:

- If you're an engineer, your typical causes are *tools* and *procedures.*
- If you're an entrepreneur, *goods* and *services.*
- If you're a politico, *laws* and *slogans.*
- If you're a soldier, *tactics* and *weapons.*
- If you're a health care worker, *therapies* and *medicines.*
- If you're a novelist or screenwriter, *characters* and *storyworlds.*

From this real-world vantage, creation can be the making of new tools, goods, laws, tactics, therapies, characters, etc. Or it can be the finding of new uses for old tools, goods, laws, tactics, therapies, characters, etc.

Selection, meanwhile, is ranking the effects of those tools, goods, characters, etc. If one tool saws faster than another, it earns the higher score for quick construction. If one character generates more empathy than another, it earns the higher score for sentimental fiction.

Since the physical world is in continual flux, driven by conflict between asymmetric life-forms, such rankings aren't absolute. They're based upon performance at a given task. A hammer can be ranked above a saw when it comes to driving nails, while a saw can be ranked above a hammer when it comes to shaping wood.

This means that there can be no ultimate tool, tactic, medicine, or screenplay. Nor can there even be a *better* tool, tactic, medicine, or screenplay, because what is handy now can in five minutes be unworkable—and what is rubbish in my cultural niche can be treasure in yours.

Yet even though we can't manufacture perfect story-thoughts, we can nonetheless cultivate better storythinking— *better* in the practical sense of being more effective and efficient (or, in biological terms, generating more growth at lower suffering and waste).

That improvement can be achieved in three broad ways: maximizing creation, honing selection, and separating creation and selection.

Here's the basics of each.

Maximizing Creation

Creation is enlarged by a focus on what *could work*. And what *could work* is enlarged by emphasizing the *specific potential* of each individual cause.

Or, to put it in ordinary language, we can maximize our brain's creativity by looking at a given tool, good, law, tactic, therapy, or character—and focusing on what makes it *unique*.

To identify that uniqueness, ask: What can this cause do that no other cause can? What's peculiar, particular, or exclusive about its function?

Once you've got your mind in the habit of emphasizing the singularity of individual causes (the opposite of Campbell's method of abstracting into general types), you can generate more *could work* via three techniques:

(1) *Work backward from effects.* Start by imagining what you want to do. Then imagine a behavior or tool that can accomplish that end, reverse-engineering from a new effect to an original cause. This reverse-engineering functions better when you stay specific, pinpointing exactly what you want to achieve and inventing a cause that achieves *only that effect*. (If you instead imagine a cause that can accomplish multiple effects, you'll drift toward magical thinking and its omnipotent causes: God, symbolism, and the philosopher's stone.)

(2) *Hybridize causes.* This is the technique beneath sexual reproduction, genetic recombination, and other biological procedures for increasing functional diversity. Use it to mix and match preexisting practices and tool uses to generate new actions, like when you marry chara‹

behaviors from one story with world opportunities from another. For this technique to be effective, don't hybridize structures, that is, products. Hybridize causal agents, that is, processes.

(3) *Maintain an inclusive library.* An inclusive library allows for conservation. Conservation is often reserved for tools and tactics that have a history of great achievement, earning them a place in the canon of classic inventions and discoveries. But conservation should also be used to keep around old tools and tactics that *didn't* succeed. Those past losers have as much potential as past winners—and possibly more. That's because, like a Michelangelo born into an era without a Sistine Chapel, they haven't found their milieu . . . yet. By hanging on to these unrealized Renaissance makers, you can rescue tomorrow's potential from today's short-term pressures, safeguarding alternative futures for when we really need them.

Join these techniques with an attitude of open-mindedness. Remind yourself that no action is intrinsically better than any other and that the future is permanently uncertain. These two biological realities mean that any cause (no matter how weird or apparently unfeasible) could supply you with the power to handle life's next twist.

Honing Selection

Selection is honed by a precise sense of the *needed result.* The more precise your sense, the faster and less wasteful your selection process.

To achieve that clarity, ask yourself: What's the minimum successful outcome? Not: What's the best possible outcome? Not: What other things would I like to accomplish? Simply and purely: What's the bare threshold of victory? What single event constitutes success?

That honing can be sharpened via three techniques:

(1) *Design tightly controlled experiments.* Do what scientists do: eliminate variables, isolating the effect of every tested action. Measure exactly what each cause is doing, so you can confidently determine which of your tools, laws, characters, etc., are working—and how.

(2) *Reject optimization for good enough.* Optimization is the goal of logic and its outputs (like critical and convergent thinking), but outside the timeless zone of mathematical idealism, it's a dangerous pursuit. To seek the optimal in any dynamic, asymmetrically contested environment is to invite catastrophic fragility. Why? Because the environmental niche to which you have perfectly adapted can at any moment go sideways, shattering your honed ideal. Better to maintain your overall flexibility by specializing only to the degree required to get by. So, when selecting, focus exclusively on what you need, not what you want. (Reserve what you want for the earlier, creation phase of storythinking.)

(3) *Prioritize second-generation outcomes.* In natural selection, the finish line isn't having children. It's having children *who themselves have children.* That's sustainable achievement. That's balancing the short-term with the long, and it's the minimum for biological success. Success isn't success if it sacrifices tomorrow for today.

Join these techniques with an attitude of detached ruthlessness toward your creations. For your grandchildren to bloom, you must weed your sons and daughters.

Separating Creation from Selection

Creation and selection have fundamentally opposite actions. That opposition is narratively generative, but logically it seems inefficient. The temptation can therefore be to subordinate either creation or selection to the other, smoothing irrational clash into harmony.

Such "improvement" will ruin your evolutionary process, replacing the fruitful antagonism of natural selection with the sterile unity of Campbell's monoproduct. To carry forward nature's method and maximize innovation, you need to ward off idealism and its dream of perfect alchemy.

In practical terms, this means that you must avoid prejudging your creations. When you imagine a new tool, law, or character, don't shape or discard it based on your past experiences. That's allowing selection into your creative process, pruning the orchard before it's been watered.

It also means that you should never play favorites during selection. Once you've decided to test a storythought, treat it with the heartless impartiality with which nature treats a new life-form. Don't permit optimism—the hope of what might be—to blunt the edge of your cull. That's allowing your creative process into selection, coddling diversity instead of trusting it to fight for itself.

The more diligently you preserve this partition between creation and selection, the more the two will boost each other. Creation will yield more narrative prototypes, allowing selection to be more vigorously disinterested.

Meanwhile, selection will yield a crisper sense of each cause's unique action, allowing creation to be more specifically original.

THE BENEFITS OF IMPROVING STORYTHINKING

The three ways of improving storythinking aren't easy. Unlike Campbell's plug-and-play formula, they plunge us into the uncertain conflict of Darwin's cauldron. Splitting our brain between creation and selection, they force our thoughts to gallop simultaneously in contrary directions: optimism and realism; anything goes and must work; liberty and discipline.

So, the natural question becomes: Why bother with that head-straining labor? Why challenge ourselves to become better storythinkers? What if we have priorities other than creativity or innovation? Or what if we're not persuaded by the fact that our neurons evolved to storythink? Perhaps they did, but what does that matter? We don't need to be tied to history—or to nature. We can leave behind our ancient synapses to engineer a more rational future of Hero's Journeys.

Yes, absolutely, we can. But in any future that contains human brains or environmental instability, there will be practical benefits to storythinking. The main ones are:

- The personal benefits of physical, emotional, and mental growth.
- The social benefits of inclusive and resilient communities that maximize the biological possibilities for individual freedom, development, and achievement.

- The spiritual benefits of discovering the meaning of life. Or at least the meaning that resonates with our brain, giving us the desire to extract the most from every waking heartbeat.

For the first benefit, turn to chapter 8. For the second, chapter 9. For the third, chapter 10.

Or, keep turning the pages into all three.

8

Storythinking for Personal Growth

The quickest path to a better tomorrow is luck. Which is why luck is so wonderful—and always to be welcomed when it chances by. But while we're waiting for luck's next arbitrary visit, we can busy ourselves with a more sustainable path to better tomorrows: growth.

Growth is the action of life. It's reacting off problems and reaching toward opportunities. It's organic, creative, and nonteleological. Which is to say: it's natural, unpredictable, and branching.

Because growth is natural, it's frequently automatic, spontaneous, and insentient: grass grows, and so do bacteria, fungi, and ecosystems. Yet growth isn't limited to nonintentional processes; it can also be informed by conscious planning. That planning makes growth more rapid, diverse, and sustainable. And like all planning, it comes from storythinking.

Unlike plant growth, storythinking isn't taught in modern biology classrooms. But its method of intelligent development has been studied by an empiricist tradition that spans from Renaissance writers (such as Shakespeare) to Romantics (such as Victor Hugo) to modern psychologists (such as William James) to Progressive reformers (such as W. E. B. Du Bois).

So varied are these names and fields of inquiry that they may seem to have little, even nothing, in common; and certainly, the tradition is a loose and mostly unincorporated one, sprawling free like prairie wildflower. Yet its spontaneous ramble was neatly summed in the early twentieth century by a University of Chicago professor who, over the course of a ninety-two-year existence, wandered the tradition's main savannahs, from Shakespeare to Romanticism, modern psychology, and Progressivism.

That long-lived, wide-striding professor was John Dewey. And his summation was: *Growth is born of narrative conflict.*

THE ROOTS OF DEWEY'S THINKING

Dewey was recruited to Chicago in 1892, at a time of massive reinvention. Plucked from its original ten-acre campus on the dusty corner of 35th and Cottage Grove, the university had been transplanted to Hyde Park's garden homes and lakeshore drives by oil magnate John D. Rockefeller, who'd entrusted its future development to a youthful Baptist philologist by the name of William Rainey Harper.

Harper was an antiquarian with an innovative bent, and he felt an instinctive kinship with the thirty-two-year-old Dewey. Dewey would, Harper was certain, remake Chicago's philosophy department. Yet as it happened, Dewey went rather further than Harper anticipated. Dewey didn't just remake Chicago's department; he set about re-creating all of professional philosophy.

Professional philosophy was then in the throes of a collapse that had begun in 1859 with the publication of Charles Darwin's *On the Origin of Species*. The *Origin* had stirred naked horror in churches—and an only slightly more concealed dismay in philosophy departments. Those departments had long instituted eternal natural forms (e.g., animal and rational and man) as the foundation of logic, which they'd in turn instituted as the foundation of ontology, epistemology, and metaphysics. The perpetuity of the natural forms was therefore the stability of philosophy's whole edifice; because man was forever, so were truth and justice.

But then in the *Origin*, Darwin advanced his theory of natural selection, challenging the immutability of biological life-forms by proposing a nonrational mechanism through which species evolved—then went extinct. And although this Darwinian narrative was radically iconoclastic, it was also indisputably compelling. Reconciling the natural world's complexities with greater elegance than any logic textbook, it explained why dinosaur fossils existed, why Australia and Argentina differed in their fauna, and why the anatomy of man contained so many animal vestiges, from the tail stump of his coccyx bone to the panic, hate, and anger of his primordial heart.

Thus did Darwin's origin story of man crumble logic's timeless cornerstone. And thus did tumble truth and justice and the rest of philosophy's cathedral architecture.

So total was this disaster that it seemed to many a philosopher that logic had run its course. If philosophy was to help humanity regain a higher permanence, it would have to do so via the intuition of the New England Transcendentalists, the faith of Søren Kierkegaard, or some other extrarational source.

But logic was not finished. Although it had barely changed since Aristotle, it would in Darwin's century develop two remarkable new forms, each of which kindled the hope that philosophy could follow the example of man—and evolve.

LOGIC'S TWO NEW FORMS

One of the new forms was Gottlob Frege's *Begriffsschrift*, or *Concept-Script: A formula language, modeled on arithmetic, for pure thought.*

Published in 1879, this ambitious book strove to covert human language into math. Words and grammar would become arithmetic symbols and equations, a transmutation that promised not only to debug human communication but also to perfect intelligence by reducing verbal conceptions (that is, the thoughts consciously articulated in human heads) to a rigorous calculus.

With this grand plan, Frege boldly advanced logic's ancient syntax. Flexing beyond Aristotle's *Organon* and its rigidly narrow utterances—*all men are rational and Achilles is a man, therefore Achilles is rational*—Frege's concept-script captured supple and extensive arrangements of subjects, predicates, and quantities: *Most people are capable of reasoned behavior, but Odysseus is the rare master of logic who is almost always rational, while Achilles is unusually emotional about military trophies.*

This breakthrough had massive implications for philosophy, yet as great an innovator as Frege was, he failed in his goal of replacing natural language with mathematical equations. Just like Aristotle, millennia before, he collided with the problem of action verbs (see chapter 5). Action verbs express action, and since action isn't timeless, it couldn't be translated into the perpetual *is* of mathematics, forcing Frege to limit his concept-script to nouns, adjectives, and linking verbs.

It was to address this limit that the second new form of logic was devised. Its devisor was the German Idealist Georg Wilhelm Friedrich Hegel, who in 1816 published his own ambitious book: *Wissenschaft der Logik—Science of Logic*. Because Hegel was writing six decades prior to Frege, he was unaware of the gap in Frege's concept-script, but he'd spotted the same hole in Aristotle.

Aristotle was revered by Hegel as history's greatest philosopher, more brilliant even than Hegel's first idol, Plato. At the root of Hegel's reverence lay his admiration for Aristotle's syllogisms, which (like the schoolmen of ancient Byzantium, golden age Baghdad, and medieval Paris) Hegel saw as infallible, the very stuff of God's eternal Reason. Yet as much as Hegel admired Aristotle's logic, he realized that it had overlooked something: biological change. Outside the logician's window, the forest's green stretched upward, and inside the logician's chest, the heart's blood pumped around. Such physical activities weren't states of *being*; they were processes of *becoming* (or, in Hegel's German, *Werden*). And *becoming* wasn't reducible to the syllogism's immortal present tense. For logic to fully comprehend the world, capturing not just the immutable heaven that God inhabited but the temporal earth that God had made below, it therefore needed to be enlarged. Aristotle's ageless identities had to be joined to a logical apparatus that could encompass life's dynamic to and fro.

That apparatus, Hegel concluded, was dialectic. Dialectic's most famous formula is *thesis-antithesis-synthesis* (see chapter 2), but dialectic can involve any two opposite entities that generate a third. In the case of *becoming*, the opposites are *being* and *nothing*, which in Hegel's logic produce a struggle that carries life—like a sprouting acorn—from immaturity into the completeness of its intended form. From nature into Godhead; from dialectic into syllogism.

The new logics of Hegel and Frege were so revolutionary that they at first produced more bewilderment than innovation, yet eventually, forward progress came. Frege's concept-script was elevated by Bertrand Russell to the foundation of analytic philosophy, whence it helped inspire rational choice economics, game theory, computer AI, and the logical infrastructures of twenty-first-century business, government, and public education. Meanwhile, Hegel's dialectic birthed Marxism and much of modern continental philosophy.

And it also wended its way to Dewey.

DEWEY GOES DIALECTIC—AND BEYOND

In 1881, Dewey was a recent college grad, kicking about his home state of Vermont, teaching elementary school from Monday to Friday and browsing philosophy journals on Saturdays. Energized by both pursuits, he decided in the spring of 1882 to find a way to pair them. And after locating a luggage trunk big enough to transport both his weekend reading and his weekday syllabi, he journeyed south to pursue a doctorate at Johns Hopkins University.

At Hopkins, Dewey encountered one of history's most brilliant logicians, C. S. Peirce. But deeming Peirce too "mathematical," Dewey immersed himself instead in Hegel's dialectic, excited by its promise to map life's dynamic character.

So compelling did Dewey find Hegel's dialectic that, had it been twenty-five years earlier, he might have become a committed Romantic. The intervening quarter century had, however, birthed Darwin's *Origin*, a copy of which sat in the Hopkins philosophy library. And upon reading the narrative of natural selection, Dewey had an epiphany: Hegel had underplayed the problem with logic. The problem wasn't that logic could not process change; the problem was that logic *locked change on a fixed route*. On that route, change could proceed toward the ideal, or it could regress, away. The former was growth; the latter decay. But within logic's timeless rule domain, change couldn't itself change. It was always just forward and back, a train chugging up and down a perpetual track.

This invariant locomotion had prompted Aristotle to make life teleological: every living thing—every acorn, every human child—was in his view programmed to grow into a predetermined archetype. And it prompted Hegel's new logic of dialectic to do the same. According to dialectic, *becoming* was a logically mandated stage on the way to *being*. It was a beating heart destined to culminate in a perfect pulse, like an electrocardiogram paused as an ideal waveform inside the algebraic mind of God.

Such plotted idealism was attractive emotionally to Dewey. But he saw immediately that its logic had been sundered by Darwin's *Origin*, which replaced teleology with the revelation that living species were forking, endlessly, to nowhere. To logic this was terrifying, because it meant the end of a permanent *is*. But to life, Dewey realized, it could be emancipating. It freed biological creatures from absolute hierarchies of value and meaning, and in doing so it also liberated language, releasing "rational" and "man" from the cage of eternal signification. Rather than being impelled to function as semiotic truths, these words could now operate as artisanal tools: useful ways of telling stories, crafting laws, and conversing about ethics.

Yet even as Dewey embraced this Darwinian revolution of philosophy, he didn't cast away everything he'd gleaned from reading Hegel. Reaching into the rubble of Hegelian dialectic, he rescued one of its core innovations: the action of growth.

GROWTH FROM HEGEL TO DEWEY

In Hegel's logic, "growth" is a synonym for "becoming." It's the process of life, the activity of living.

Hegel wasn't the first philosopher to emphasize growth; growth had played an important role in Aristotle's metaphysics. But Hegel nevertheless added a twist: where Aristotle had seen mental and physical development as upshots of natural algorithms, Hegel treated them as products of a collision between antagonistic elements. In Hegel's logic, growth thus stopped being a computational output. And it became the offspring of conflict.

This Hegelian dynamic of growth out of conflict excited Dewey for a reason that Hegel could not have imagined: it offered a way to reframe the most troubling aspect of Darwin's new science. According to that science, life had come about for no reason and was headed to no particular destination, making it battle for the sake of battle, unending and without purpose. Such pointless violence was dismaying to the human brain, which is why even Darwin's acolytes supported him reluctantly. They didn't want (any more than Darwin himself had wanted) for nature to be aimless war; they simply felt that the only intellectually honest option afforded by the *Origin*'s hard science was to accept the fundamental tragedy of lived existence.

But then, in Hegel's claim that struggle could generate growth, Dewey saw a way to invest Darwinian conflict with purpose. That purpose wasn't the logical one of Aristotelian nature or Hegelian dialectic, yet it possessed its own coherent mechanism: narrative. Like a story, it was generated by conflict. And like a story, it was psychologically resonant not because it contained permanent truths but because it provided the experience of discovering new possibilities for life activity, stimulating intense feelings of wonder, hope, and meaning.

Dewey began outlining this narrative natural philosophy in an 1898 *Monist* essay, "Evolution and Ethics," which flipped the title of a lecture—"Ethics and Evolution"—delivered five years earlier by Thomas Henry Huxley. Huxley was a staunch defender of Darwin's theory of natural selection, so staunch that he earned himself the moniker "Darwin's bulldog." Yet despite that hard-won public reputation, Huxley had deep misgivings about Darwinism's moral consequences, and in his lecture, he'd declared that humanity's ultimate goal was to evolve beyond evolution, replacing nature's blind cruelty with cultivated charity: "the practice of that which is ethically best—what we call goodness or virtue—involves a course of conduct which, in all respects, is opposed to that which leads to success in the cosmic struggle for existence."

This pivot out of nature was intended to repudiate social Darwinism and eugenics, two pseudoscientific distortions of Darwin's theory that appalled Huxley—and also Dewey. But while Dewey shared Huxley's abhorrence of attempts to engineer a master race, he was also perturbed by Huxley's anti-Darwinian alternative. In fact, Huxley's ethics struck Dewey as so unbiological that in his own lecture, he condemned it as literally antilife: "The man who regards his animal inheritance as evil in and of itself apart from its relation to aims proposed by his intelligence, has logically but one recourse,—to seek Nirvana. With him the principle of self-negation becomes absolute."

In place of Huxley's life-ending immaterialism, Dewey pivoted into a narrative of growth:

> The growth of science, its application in invention to industrial life, the multiplication and acceleration of means of transportation and intercommunication, have created a peculiarly unstable environment. . . . In [that] environment, flexibility of function, the enlargement of the range of uses to which one and the same organ, grossly considered, may be put, is a great, almost the supreme, condition of success. As such, any change in that direction is a favorable variation which must be selected.

Evolution's upshot was thus to increase life's "flexibility of function," or in other words, to do the opposite of what

Huxley had claimed. Rather than culminating in an optimally enlightened life-form (the human race) that broke from nature by devising eternal rules of right and wrong, evolution was a ceaseless process of selecting variants that contained more potential for variation. Hence our species had evolved the open-ended tools of opposable thumbs, plotting brains, and modern science, all of which had as their basic function the enlarging of options for future activity. The human cultures that Huxley had taken as proof of evolution's obsolescence were instead evidence that evolution encouraged an ethics that did intentionally what natural selection had done unintentionally: grow life's capacity to act more diversely.

With this rethinking of Darwinian evolution, Dewey rebooted his Chicago university department—and the rest of professional philosophy. Trading the metaphysical ideal of eternal signification for a physical method of diversifying function, he reframed conflict from a *logical problem* (to be solved via synthesis, abstraction, or rational decision making) into a *narrative opportunity* (for personal growth). The result was an ethics that harnessed struggle as a source of cultural and scientific innovation, leveraging the oppositions between divergent lives into practical ways to grow better at growing.

The rich possibilities for this evolutionary ethics can be gleaned from Dewey's Romantic precursors: Johann Goethe, Victor Hugo, Charles Delacroix, Vincent van Gogh, and other philosopher-artists who sought an alternative to Enlightenment logic in the vivacious clashes of Shakespearean drama. And more still of its possibilities can be gained from Dewey's followers: Progressive educators and psychologists such as Du Bois, Ronald Salmon Crane, and Martin Seligman.

But while these possibilities are all worth exploring, we can, for summary purposes here, distill them to a single narrative process: harnessing conflict to generate personal growth of three kinds—physical, emotional, and intellectual.

THE THREE KINDS OF PERSONAL GROWTH

Physical Growth. Physical growth is generated by the conflict between our mind and our body. That conflict is inherent and automatic, but, like any narrative process, it can be rendered more fruitful by intentional storythinking (see chapter 7), yielding a three-part recipe for growing our physical range of motion:

1. Listen with our mind to our body's current range of motion, that is, our body's existing physical narratives.
2. Use those narratives not to define what our body *is* but to speculate on what our body *could do.*
3. Convert those speculations into fresh narratives for our body to try.

To help our body attempt those fresh narratives, our mind can act like a dance partner, encouraging our body to push beyond its comfort zone without going so far that it tumbles. Our mind can, in short, have more confidence in our body than our body has in itself, because our mind can perceive, as our body cannot, our body's potential to do what it has never done before.

▶ ▷ ▶

Emotional Growth. Emotional growth builds on the narrative action of physical growth. It occurs when our mind challenges our heart to attempt new behaviors that bring more of the things our heart wants for itself. This interactive mind-heart struggle yields flexible stories for nurturing mental health (by reducing negative emotions such as grief, trauma, anger, loneliness, and pessimism) and well-being (by promoting positive emotions such as wonder, purpose, joy, love, courage, and gratitude).

The flexibility of this process manifests in the way we may discover that in one moment of setback, we can ward off an anxiety spiral by telling ourselves: *That was just bad luck. It wasn't something intrinsic in me that caused that disaster.* While we may discover that in another moment of setback, it's empowering to tell ourselves the opposite tale: *That was my fault. I caused that, and I will learn. I have the confidence in myself, and the healthy belief in my own powers of self-determination, to take full ownership of this disaster—even if there are signs that there were other factors at work.*

And these two stories are themselves just a fraction of the branching options for leveraging life's downs and ups into sources of emotional resilience and positive emotion. There exists in global literature a vast library of narratives for growing our hardiness and our joy, a library that our storytelling brain can daily expand with never-before-seen characters and plots. Because every heart is different, and every situation varies. There's no universal right or wrong for therapy or thriving.

▶ ▷ ▶

Intellectual Growth. Intellectual growth is supported by emotional and physical growth, because our mind is really not a mind. It is a brain. And the more emotionally and physically healthy our brain, the more its higher intellectual operations can grow.

That intellectual growth can branch in endless directions, but they all have one thing in common: they expand our brain's range of actions, allowing it to adapt better to life's obstacles and opportunities. Intellectual growth's core biological function is thus to increase our creative planning, expanding the diversity, elaborateness, and originality of our storythinking.

Intellectual growth is generated via the same narrative process as physical and emotional growth, with one twist: instead of challenging our body or heart, our mind must challenge itself.

This self-challenging requires our mind to split apart. Such splitting is logically paradoxical but psychologically straightforward; our brain's perspective-shifting networks enable it to imagine itself as different characters who envision unique challenges and opportunities—and therefore unique plot possibilities—in nature's storyworlds (see chapter 2). The result is an inner theater in which our mind, like a Shakespearean drama, tussles one potential course of action against another, generating fresh behavioral scripts for us to try.

Those new scripts expand the ways that our mind can challenge our body and heart, so just as physical and emotional growth give to intellectual growth, it returns to them, feeding the creative passions and practices that inspire new technologies, new works of art, new political platforms, new scientific hypotheses, new social movements, new business plans, new schemes for the day. And intellectual growth can also be its own end. It provides the thrill of mental freedom and stimulates the possibility thinking that's our brain's highest biological purpose—and the day's always opportunity.

At which point, once our mind has done all it can to grow itself, the next question becomes: Can we grow further? Can we go beyond personal growth into social growth, stretching into intellectual communities that expand life's potential wider and higher than the imaginations of lone storythinkers?

Yes. As we'll explore in the next chapter, we can.

9

Storythinking for Social Growth

Where does society come from? And does it support our individuality? Or constrain it?

These are thorny questions. So thorny that they've pricked just about every thinker who's dared to touch them. But still, a promising start toward answers was made many years ago in a wintry suburb of sixteenth-century Florence, where amid frosted wheat fields sat the bad inn, an irregular brick domicile with a cellar escape tunnel, in case the prince's gangsters came knocking again.

THE BAD INN

It was December 10, 1513.

Hunched over a desk in the inn's clay murk was forty-three-year-old Niccolò Machiavelli. He'd been exiled there eight months earlier from his birthplace of Florence, although the city remained close enough that, in the quiet of evenlight, he could hear the laughter of its *piazza* revelers. The sound was painful, a match for the memory of the gangsters breaking his shoulders with rope. But shrugging it off, Machiavelli dipped a quill in iron ink to record the story of his new life in the countryside: "I hunt sparrows and truck lumber until dusk falls. Then I return home and enter my study. At the door, I trade my muddied robes for my finest clothes. Now dressed fitly, I step into the courts of ancient men, where, lovingly welcomed, I feed on that food for which I was born. I ask the men the reason for their actions [*ragione delle loro azioni*]; and from their humanity, they answer."

By chatting like this with the past, Machiavelli seemed to set a backward course. Yet in a plot swerve that made him famous, his question-and-answer sessions guided him to join an original-minded group that he dubbed *innovatori*—innovators.

Innovators were makers of new laws. Which is to say, they were the inventors of fresh rules for social action. They included, in Machiavelli's opinion, the Hebrew prophet Moses and the founders of Rome's republic, but their specific identities were less important than the greater fact they demonstrated: the ethical insufficiency of logic. Logic had led the medieval Church to conclude that morality was timeless, meaning, in turn, that every good deed had already been instantiated by God. From the Church's pious perspective, any novel rule of action was thus, by definition, evil, as illustrated by Eve's original sin in Eden.

Machiavelli disagreed. In the example of the *innovatori*, he saw the proof that inventive social actions could change human life for the good. And at the same desk, during the same year that he narrated his country life in exile, he expressed his enthusiasm for innovation in what would become his most notorious treatise: *Il Principe—The Prince.*

The Prince was its own form of innovation: in place of the rational doctrines of medieval political philosophy, it offered a storywork of stratagems. And of those stratagems, the grand exemplar was *The Prince* itself: plotted to gain the prince's favor by proving that its author could scheme as cynically as any gangster, it was a cunning gambit to vault Machiavelli out of the bad inn and back into Florence.

The gambit failed. The prince was unimpressed by *The Prince*, marooning Machiavelli at his gloomy desk. Yet the exile did not abandon hope. He continued back-and-forthing with the ancients, taking as his next conversation partner the Latin historian Livy. Livy had been born in Padua sixteen centuries earlier, 120 miles north of the bad inn. He'd spent his early years in his own country retreat, avoiding partisan politics and civil war, until in middle age, he'd left home to pen what he saw as history's greatest story: Rome, from backwater birth to Caesarian empire.

The result was an epic 142-book chronicle that stretched from the mythic age when Trojan refugees had founded a new city in Italy all the way to the day that Livy himself sat in that city, marveling at its imperial wealth. Such was the chronicle's narrative bulk that later archivists grew weary of transcribing its contents, abridging them into summaries before at last surrendering the job entirely. By Machiavelli's day, only about a quarter of the original survived, the rest disintegrated into papyrus dust or nibbled up by library moths.

Still, in the fragments, Machiavelli could detect Livy's voice. And each night after he returned from the fields to don his closet finery, he asked that voice: *What was the reason for your actions? And what, do you think, were the reasons for the actions of the lives who came before?*

The answers were surprising, unlike anything that either Machiavelli or Livy had previously writ. So, to preserve their original genius, Machiavelli procured a fresh stack of parchment. He titled it *Discorsi di Tito Livio—Conversations with Livy*. And on its rippled leaves, he recorded a plan for inventing better stratagems.

Stratagems that didn't involve princes. But instead, free societies.

130 THE FREE-SOCIETY BLUEPRINT

Conversations with Livy is studied now in universities across the world as a contribution to political philosophy. Just as medieval scholastics at Oxford and Paris mined Aristotle's *Politics* for insights into ideal kingdoms, so have modern scholars sifted Machiavelli's parchment for the founding principles of republicanism, treating it as a text that contains a well-reasoned thesis—perhaps even the final truth—about the origins and operations of free societies.

By doing so, those scholars have diligently, earnestly, and completely missed the point. *Conversations* isn't a rational inquiry into the principles of good government. It's a series of non sequiturs and outright reversals. The preface begins with Machiavelli announcing his plan to innovate by reviving the ancients, a paradoxical assertion that leads rapidly to more:

- *Conversations'* first chapter describes Rome as a city of destiny whose success was evident from its origin. The second chapter then describes Rome as precisely the opposite: a beneficiary of enormous fortune, obtaining by chance what its founders failed to design.
- *Conversations'* first book builds to the grand oxymoron: "Here we see the Roman Senate's steadfast virtue: how always, no matter what, it wasn't ashamed to reject its previous behavior." Or in other words: the Senate was regularly irregular, an institution that consistently swerved.
- *Conversations'* second book starts with Machiavelli observing that he seems to have contradicted himself. At which point, he disputes his own observation—before plunging into further contradictions.

131

As rationally perplexing as these switchbacks are, they have a straightforward motive: Machiavelli doesn't believe in timeless reasons that can be followed in all cases. He thinks that every situation has unique contours, necessitating plastic politics: "Actions—especially big ones—must be adapted to the moment. To act against the moment—whether because of psychological compulsion or our own free choice—is to doom ourselves to misery and failure." Hence it is that Machiavelli celebrates freedom—yet also dictators. Hence it is that Machiavelli reveres piety—yet is frankly irreligious. Hence it is that Machiavelli inveighs against factional conflict—yet credits the factional conflict between nobles and plebs for Rome's political greatness.

This flexibility is responsible for Machiavelli's notorious reputation as an arch-pragmatist. And it hatches another riddle: What practical advice can be provided by a book that claims that anything goes, so long as the situation is propitious? Isn't *Conversations* just a long-winded insistence that success boils down to happenstance? And isn't that the same as saying that there's no foreseeable way to engineer better societies, only canny rationalizations pieced together after the fact?

In short, isn't political instrumentalism intrinsically devoid of practical direction?

Mathematically, yes. Machiavelli's contradictions add up to nothing. (Literally: X plus its opposite equals zero.) Yet even though *Conversations* lacks logical substance, it's still able to provide useful guidance through another intellectual mechanism: narrative.

Narrative is everywhere in *Conversations*, which recapitulates Livy's origin story of Rome, made vivid with historical fables: "There's the famous tale of Horatius Cocles holding off an army . . . and of Cincinnatus plowing his little field . . . and of the public's onetime hero, Manlius Capitolinus." These legendary anecdotes are entwined with a relentless emphasis on narrative's nonlogical engine of cause and effect—"*the cause of this was . . . the cause of that was*"—all of which builds to the plot twist: "Thus it comes about that republics survive better and enjoy good fortune longer than princedoms. Because the diversity of their people allows them to adapt better to the diversity of the times." This is easy to misread as a rational maxim: *republics > princedoms*. But it's another logic buster. In the narrative of *Conversations*, what makes republics into republics is diversity. And diversity isn't a perfectible attribute. Unlike unity (the defining attribute of princedoms), diversity has no eternal endpoint, no ideal culmination. It can always be increased, not simply in quantity but in quality: there are endless ways to think and do different.

That illimitable space for growth is why Machiavelli declares that the ultimate source of political success is innovation. And while this emphasis on creative action leads to another logical dead end (there can be no calculus of novelty, no algorithm for originality), a door forward is once again opened by story. Story reveals that Machiavelli's account of republics isn't a timeless truth but a historical opportunity: republics have come about haphazardly over time yet have done better than mere chance allows, stumbling into a set of behaviors that work more reliably than rational alternatives. And although this lucky strike can't be computationally replicated, it can be continued by feeding the narrative process that birthed it. Which is to say, by retelling the story of past republics, we can keep alive the actions of their characters, extending Rome's tale through our own sequels.

Such extension is what *Conversations* encourages. Instead of anointing itself the final word on politics, it invites us to do what Machiavelli did when he read Livy and keep the story going: "The work of my narrative isn't done yet. But helped on by others, I've carried it far enough that I believe that it won't be too hard for someone else to get it there." This invitation to carry on the plot would be accepted by many later storythinkers, branching into future tales of communal science, liberty, and ethics:

- In the 1620s, Francis Bacon elaborated Machiavelli's *Conversations* into *New Atlantis*, a utopian parable that imagines a "diverse" collective of empiricists inventing "diverse" solutions to life's "diverse" problems.

133

- In 1762, Jacques-Jean Rousseau expanded Machiavelli's *Conversations* into the populist narrative of *The Social Contract*: "Men are born free yet are everywhere in chains."
- In 1776, Thomas Paine spun Machiavelli's *Conversations* into the revolutionary inclusiveness of *Common Sense*: "I fully and conscientiously believe . . . that there should be a diversity of religious opinions among us."

And if we want, we can now join the plot ourselves.

JOINING THE PLOT

134 Last chapter, we identified Dewey's method of personal growth: an experimental feedback loop between our storythinking brain and the rest of our anatomy. Machiavelli's method of social growth is the same, but with one innovation: the experimental feedback loop is between our storythinking brain and . . . *another* storythinking brain. It's two of us storythinkers, hooked up together.

By connecting ourselves in this way, we operate as one another's laboratory audiences, nurturing each other's potential for innovation by encouraging improvisational actions that are shaped through empirical reinforcement. So, like characters in a novel, we come together in an original plot that extends the story longer, through more chances for narrative branching, than a script that centers on one hero's journey, alone.

In practical terms, this social experiment is launched when we reverse the behavior of princes. Rather than telling people what they should do in the future, we ask them: "Why did you do what you did in the past?" Such is the specific question—[*Qual è la*] *ragione delle loro azioni?*—that Machiavelli directed toward the ancients as he sat at his desk in the bad inn.

When we pose this question without judgment to our fellow citizens, we gain access to the psychological motives—that is, the biological causes—at the bottom of their behaviors, enabling us to explore what they *might* (not *should*) do in the future. Out of that exploration will come a wending conversation that generates possibilities for action that neither of our minds would have imagined alone. And at the same time as we're helping our fellow citizens grow their creative suite of future options, they can return the favor by asking us about our own past behaviors, evolving our range of motion in tandem.

This process of mutual growth yields a freedom very different from that of classical liberalism. In classical liberalism (and its libertarian offspring), freedom is a logically immutable right that, like the laws of mathematics, has always been (and will always be) true. According to that everlasting principle, society is the product of individuals who voluntarily come together, forming contracts to secure their wealth and extend their life spans. It's a rational decision, made out of mutual self-interest, designed to maintain the good that already *is*.

Storythinking offers a counternarrative: it's not individuals that create democratic society, but democratic society that creates individuals. This isn't logical, but it unfolds as a straightforward sequence of biological actions: in the beginning, back in a state of nature, you and I weren't individuals; we were each a whole society unto ourself, responsible for an entire nation's work. I did all my food making, all my protecting, all my clothing, all my

135

entertaining. And so did you. You played the roles of farmer, soldier, tailor, playwright. You, alone, were everyone in your empire.

But then we met each other and saw a chance to specialize. If we joined together, I could be the farmer and you, the soldier. And the more people we invited into our communal narrative, the more specialization could occur. To my farming and your soldiering, we added tailors and playwrights—and from there we kept adding until at last, we had multiple kinds of clothiers and entertainers, each with their own stitching and performance methods. Thus our society enabled us to become individuals, trading our do-everything lifestyles for unique civic roles.

This narrative process generates the diversity of action that makes republics more resilient—and more prosperously happy. And it also generates something else: trust. Trust is the emotional result of both perspective shifting and collaboration, so it forms part of the connective tissue of republics, tightening the ties between individuals and holding the broader public together.

And the wonder of this process is that it doesn't just bond society through trust. Because this process is narrative, it can also generate cohesion through another mechanism: conflict.

THE SOCIAL GLUE OF NARRATIVE CONFLICT

Conflict is a counterintuitive source of cohesion, but it binds stories for a simple reason: conflict isn't just one actor fighting against another; it's also one actor fighting *with* another. That *with* sticks the actors together: to win the conflict, they must continue engaging their opponent. Which is why narrative conflict tends to perpetuate itself. As long as two characters in a story remain at odds, there will be a sequel.

In the case of republics, conflict is lent additional stick by the fact that the struggle is over a special commodity: freedom. To call freedom a commodity is to acknowledge: it is made. It's not an innate right, handed us by Reason or Nature. It comes into being when societies (via the storythinking narrative above) liberate us from the burden of doing everything we need to survive. The moment I become a farmer, you're freed from the need to sow crops. The moment you become a tailor, I'm relieved of the obligation to sew clothes. And the more such specialization proceeds, the more liberation occurs: you and I don't need to make soap, cornmeal, shoes, songs, tables, or a million other things. We can be released to devote our time to tasks—and hobbies—that suit our personal inclinations.

This freedom is the most prized commodity of republics. Partly, that's because the alternative—being forced to work—is unpleasant and dispiriting. But mostly, it's because the opportunity to plot our own lives is empowering and fun, giving us a constant appetite for additional liberties. Which means that we spend most of our time in republics jousting with our fellow citizens over who gets to be more free.

That jousting is the jousting we do over specialized social roles. If I want my role to be gadget making, I'll naturally be thrust into competition with everyone else who's trying to become a professional engineer; if I want my role to be theater production, I'll naturally be thrust into competition with everyone else who's trying to recruit actors and audiences. Such competition doesn't always take the form of open aggression; we can learn from our rivals and even, when the social prospects are open enough, mentor one another. But at some point the opportunity space will tighten, and we'll feel the pinch to win. So, we'll bend all our ingenuity, all our resources, and all our will to defeating the person whose special social role is most like ours.

From the perspective of individuals, this conflict is brutal. It can dash hopes and end careers, and it's characterized throughout by painful emotional urgency. Because freedom is a cherished psychological good, we can experience terrible angst when others outdo us in our chosen field. Yet even so, the conflict is a contributor to social growth, for two reasons:

1. The conflict promotes further specialization. Since you and I cannot easily succeed if we're both doing the same thing, it pushes each of us to seek the distinctive potential of our nature, developing original-to-us behaviors that secure our place in the jostle to live uninhibited. Which is to say: the conflict encourages me to develop my personal gadget-making capabilities, and you, yours, increasing our individual odds of survival and also opening the possibility that, if our capabilities are different enough, we can survive together.

2. The conflict's destructive force is limited. That's because our freedoms are mutually interdependent: the more social diversity exists, the more I'm free to do my own thing. So, broadly speaking, none of us gains in the long term by acting tyrannically: if I control others, restricting their growth, I lose out on the freedom that their growth would create for

me. And although each of us is liable—even prone—to fits of pettiness in which we seek to crush our rivals, society as a whole has a vested interest in preventing such damage. If I, in my zealousness to run the only drama troupe in town, set fire to your theater, I destroy everyone else's freedom to enjoy two types of entertainment (or to audition for two types of play). And if you respond to my arson by demanding that I be hanged, you diminish the same freedoms, which is why republics work organically over time to install checks against conflict's extreme consequences, maximizing its function as a source of innovation and togetherness.

This social maximization of innovation and togetherness does to narrative what computer AI does to logic: scales it. Just as AI can solve computational problems faster than a lone logician, so can storythinking communities plot actions more creatively than a lone storythinker—making good on Machiavelli's claim that republics are better at the practical process of adapting to life's changing tides.

And bringing this book near to its ending.

THIS BOOK'S ENDING

This book began by pledging to restore the partnership between story and thinking that ancient sages, in the days before Plato, marshalled to tackle humanity's primordial question: *How can I make my life better?*

Perhaps the previous chapters have made good on that promise. Perhaps they've shone light on the narrative gears of human intelligence. Perhaps they've explained how those gears can power personal and social growth, helping you plan your own storythinking ethics.

Or perhaps not. Perhaps they've fallen into story's old problems. Perhaps they've skipped free of data. Perhaps they've mildly entertained without seriously informing, revealing nothing more than the author's peculiar skew.

Yet either way, they've got as far down the road as they can. If their wheels have by now carried you nowhere valuable, you can confidently abandon the ride, knowing you gave it fair try. And if the journey is worth continuing, it has made enough headway for you to reach the next mile marker on your own.

But even if you can spot that marker, you might not be feeling particularly eager to continue. In fact, you might be feeling eager's opposite: apathetic. Because now that we've gone as far as we've gone, you can see that the book in your hands has neglected something quite important.

Okay, not *quite* important. *Very* important. *Crucially* important. The book has gone all this distance, through all these chapters, without bothering to explain the point of going at all. Or phrased more philosophically, the book has acted—out of foolishness or laziness—as if human life's root question is: *How* do I live? When, really, the question is: *Why?*

Why is the thing that gets us up in the morning—and the thing that impels us, throughout all the day's trials, to keep on trying. *Why* is the reason that we choose each dawn to live, to not give up, to carry on the hard adventure.

Why isn't a problem for most living things, because most living things are propelled automatically. They operate as machines, powered by the gears of their bacterial DNA, their vegetable stalks, their animal reflexes. And much of the time, we operate that way too. Our brains are moved by our emotions: fears, hopes, desires. Their passion makes us care. Their urgency thrusts us on.

But not always. Because the human brain isn't just an engine of feeling. It's also, as we've explored over the previous chapters, an engine of planning. In the brain's earliest days, back before it was human, that planning was limited. Part of the limit came from the brain's cranial size, and part from the lack of time the brain had to cogitate: the hours were crowded, full of pressing dangers and pleasures, so planning had to be equally hasty. Yet gradually those restrictions lifted. The brain grew, developing the human neocortex. And the crush of nature was pushed back by civilization, creating whole afternoons for our brain to plot forward and back.

Thus it came to be that storythinking confronted the brain with the question: *Why* are we here? And its quick follower: *Why* keep going? There was no ultimate point that the brain could see. And in fact, the more the brain brooded, the more it began to believe that there *could be* no ultimate point. For when the brain employed its narrative cogs to fast-forward time, what it saw was: death. Death was the inevitable end of life's story. And given that inevitability, what purpose existed in striving onward?

This is the question we must face now. Why does it matter that some societies adapt better, if in the end, they suffer life's common fate: extinction? Why strive energetically to pen a communal tale when every tale must run its course, forgotten in the wake of newer narratives? Why expend our days on struggle when the struggle is—and will always be—unwinnable?

Why, in short, bother with growth at all?

141

The answer provided by biology is: because growth is our nature, and therefore good in itself. Yet this answer is really just another version of logic's old sophistry: converting an action into a being. So, in the next and final chapter, we'll explore the answer that narrative supplies.

Which is to say: we'll find story's answer to the meaning of life.

10

Story's Answer to the Meaning of Life

Sometime around 300 BCE, she exited west through the four towers of Athens's sacred gate. And walking the north bank of the Eridanus River, she arrived at the Garden.

The Garden bloomed on a small plot of land, loosely enclosed by a low wood fence. At its open door she was handed an earthen cup filled with water. And cooling her thirst, she entered to stroll among summer plum and mulberry trees.

Who she was, we can't say with certainty. We think we know her name: Leontion. We think we know her profession: a *hetaira*, or paid girlfriend, clever, charming, and willing to satisfy a man's wants; for enough cash, anything was possible, even the lifelong love of bearing his child. And we think we know why she came to the Garden: she was attached to the arm of Metrodorus of Lampsacus, an ebullient gastronomist who'd appalled Athens's most eminent philosophers, the Platonists, by declaring that wisdom dwelled in the belly.

Yet as to why she stayed in the Garden, that's a harder matter. If she'd wanted, she could have left its modest fruit and barley meals, and she could have left the arm of Metrodorus, too. Her job gave her that freedom. She wasn't trapped in a wife's chambers (upstairs, beside the sleeping quarters of the slaves), emerging only (when appropriately accompanied) to do the oyster-cake shopping and wool-tunic washing. She could wander anywhere by herself—the downstairs drinking couches, the gymnasium fields dotting the city outskirts, the theater bleachers on the southern Acropolis.

Not, of course, that her freedom was limitless. She had to feed herself, which meant finding a client, which meant, in turn, that she had to groom her hair, perfume her skin, and clothe her body in ways that agreeably surprised the senses. All that cost time, thought, and silver. And it required, too, that she compete with other eye-catchers for men's attention.

Did she like that attention? Did she enjoy the long gaze surveying her? Did she relish the emphatic pause during which a man decided whether her body was worth the drachma coins inside his fist? Probably not. Even if she passed the test, it was never pleasant to be in someone else's power, your future hanging on their verdict.

So, that's one thing she might have enjoyed about the Garden, encouraging her to linger in its green, away from the more boisterous entertainments of symposium wine flasks and phallic stage clowns. For the Garden's purpose was to create a space free from men's judgments. That space was not, admittedly, perfect; Metrodorus remained close, his maw stuffed with olives, his muscled fingers grabbing. But that the space existed at all was a credit to the creative thinking of the Garden's founder, Epicurus.

Epicurus was an Athenian born near Troy in the eastern colonies, where he'd studied the books of the atomists, a weird sect who thought that the world had been birthed not by gods or by reason but by happenstance. After developing a few equally unconventional theories of his own, Epicurus had then been expelled from the isle of Lesbos, which found even its Sapphic tolerance overtaxed by his iconoclastic life teachings. At which point he'd come here, to the outskirts of Athens, to set himself up as a philosopher.

Not that Epicurus liked being called a philosopher, mind you. He thought the philosophers talked as much twaddle as their ancient rivals: the poets. And indeed, his intent in cultivating the Garden was to provide a refuge from the twin ills of philosophy and poetry, or, to name their deeper roots, logic and story.

THE TWIN ILLS OF LOGIC AND STORY

Story's ill was the more ancient. In times long ago, it had caused humankind to imagine a sky full of angry gods, and from there, to dream that the gods were so unappeasably angry that they refused to allow us to die at our deaths but kept alive our souls in darkness to wrack us with eternal torments.

All of which, of course, was nonsense. There were no furious gods; there was no perdition beyond the grave.

And as for the ill of logic: logic had caused humankind to deduce immutable laws of right and wrong from which there could be no deviation. Deviation, the logicians claimed, led swiftly to chaos, a state of such dreadful incoherence that to avoid it, the first hint of license had to be punished by enlightened tyrants. Not to mention that some philosophers had gone still further, asserting that it was impossible for us, even if we wanted, to depart from the rules. For so deeply were the rules embedded in physics that they dictated all we did, turning us into clockworks on the track of Fate.

Which was also nonsense. Philosophical rules shouldn't be imposed by force. Nor were we prisoners of destiny. Life was free. If it wasn't, we could never be happy, for liberty was essential to mental gladness, and as proof of such gladness—and therefore of freedom—Epicurus pointed at the smiles of Leontion and the other folk who entered the Garden.

This proof provoked much smirking among the philosophers. They said: *Epicurus, all that's proved by the gladness of the Garden is that you and your friends were predestined to be glad.* Or even: *You Garden people are only superficially happy; to reach real bliss, you need my higher enlightenment.* But such naysaying was ignored by Epicurus. He devoted his energies to growing his new way: happiness. Happiness was the justification for everything done in the Garden. Any action that contributed to its increase was gently nurtured. Any action that didn't was firmly weeded.

With his cultivation of contentment, Epicurus returned philosophy to its ancient root: ethics. Ethics, as we saw in chapter 2, is the attempt to address the practical question: How can I make my life better? Which Epicurus answered, in the manner of a hedonic accountant, by teaching: forget worldly success, rich cuisine, heaven, gods, metaphysical verities, and other made-up or unreachable things that bring dissatisfaction and angst. Satisfy your natural aches—hunger, curiosity, loneliness—with simple meals, empirical facts, and honest friends. That will optimize your gladness between birth and death; that's the recipe for the best possible life span.

This utilitarian ethics earned Epicurus the ire of generations of deontic preachers, an ire that endures in our use of "epicurean" as a synonym for "glutton," "gastric fantastic," and "godless worshiper of sensuality." All of which can seem an overreaction, but alerts us to just how insurgent Epicurus was. By restoring ethics to its original place as the basis of philosophy, he disturbed metaphysics, the modern groundwork upon which the philosophers had come to rest their professional authority (see chapter 2), prompting the philosophers to set aside their comparatively minor squabbles with each other and unite with one voice to condemn Epicurus's sally against the bulwark of their rising power, wealth, and fame.

Nor were the philosophers the only guardians of metaphysics. The guardians also included many nonacademic folk who'd run into the problem we encountered at last chapter's end: the human brain's emotional need for *Why*. Yearning for a feeling of greater purpose, those folk had responded with hopeful wonderment when the philosophers had quarried *Whys* of various ideologies to install as life's new foundation. And they had come to revere philosophy's new temple architecture as fiercely as the philosophers themselves.

Yet despite such popular veneration, the philosophers' new masonry had, Epicurus concluded, failed to better the public's daily existence. Instead, its rational granite of Justice and Truth had stoked unnecessary anxieties about fantastical hells and logical principles, contravening the original purpose of ethics and hence, philosophy. So, now it was time for the metaphysical construction project to end. No longer would inner experience be subordinated to the external verities deduced by Plato's Academy, Aristotle's Lyceum, and Athens's other reigning schools. No longer would the human psyche groan beneath moral dictates and mystical prescriptions. Instead, ethics would itself be elevated into the *Why*. Happiness would become the alpha and omega, philosophy's sum total, the twilight of the gods. And it would be found, complete, in the Garden.

148

Epicurus's Garden worked. It improved many ancient Mediterranean lives, including that of Leontion. And has its acolytes still; although there aren't many self-declared Epicureans ambling among us, millions everywhere belong to the cult of happiness, chasing it as life's ultimate good.

Yet as successful as Epicurus's ethics has been, it has not succeeded completely, for two reasons:

First, our brain can only be so happy. That's because brain happiness comes from chemicals that exist in limited neural quantities, and although we can increase those quantities with opiates and other artificial substances, the increase soon produces a hangover in which our brain counterbalances our drug intake by cutting back the manufacture of our natural bliss. This cutback happens because happiness evolved (like everything in our head) not as an ideal end state but as a biological tool. That tool's function is to nurture ongoing growth, so it's valued by our brain as a temporary reward. Doled out too liberally, it would make us lazily self-satisfied, a recipe for death in the contested habitats of life.

This natural limit to happiness was discovered, via trial and error, by Epicurus. Which is why he offered water, not wine, to his visitors; why he focused on the quality, not the quantity, of joy; and why the only entertainment in his leafy enclosure was friendly conversation. But as prudent as this restrained happiness was, it couldn't overcome . . .

Second, a focus on happiness is psychologically counterproductive. This has been discovered by recent psychology research, which has shown that the more that we turn happiness into a metric, the more that we compare ourselves to others—and to ourselves. This is how metrics work, after all: they rank. Which means that our brain inevitably starts to worry: *She's happier than me.* And: *I was happier before.* Pulling down our gladness with the fret: *This isn't perfect happiness. It could be better* . . .

But even though the Garden didn't satisfy modern science's full conditions for an empirically durable ethics, it still went a good distance toward addressing the problem raised at the last chapter's end: transitioning ethics from *How* into *Why*.

So, to see if we can perhaps advance a bit further, let's return with fresh eyes to Epicurus's diagnosis of how story and logic went astray.

HOW STORY AND LOGIC WENT ASTRAY

Story, as we saw in chapter 2, predates logic, inviting us to begin our diagnosis with story's problem.

The problem, as crisply anatomized by Epicurus, is that story led our species to imagine hell. Exactly how story got us to this myth, it's impossible to say; our archives and archaeological records have captured only a few grains of history's vast hourglass. But still, we can say that hell was not there at the beginning. In the beginning, the story was simply that the world was alive. That living world was characterized variously in different stories, some of which still exist today, passed down by Brazilian rainforest tribes, East African hunter-gatherer Hadze, and Australian Indigenous Peoples.

From these enduring oral traditions, we can see that the world's aliveness first manifested itself in tales about giants, gods, and spirit folk who caused rivers, rains, and the other natural happenings that science traces now to geology, meteorology, and physics. Out of that earthly aliveness, the story then developed chapters, forward and backward. The backward chapters rolled time in reverse, detailing the causes of the gods and giants, all the way to the ultimate genesis. The forward chapters leaped ahead, imagining future ages—and then, the story's ultimate ending: Elysium, Valhalla, Fólkvangr, and other bodily paradises where the heroes of legend reveled in feasts, songs, and friends.

All this story was positive. It deepened our brain's emotional *Why* by making us feel part of a bigger narrative, filled with huge lives, headed for rapture.

But then in scattered clans and kingdoms across the archaic world, the narrative began to take a less positive turn. Warped by jealousy, anxiety, and other negative feelings, people stopped being glad for the heroes in heaven and coveted paradise themselves. To satisfy this envious yearning, up sprouted priests beside the Nile and other sacred waterways to promise: *Do as I say, and bliss will be yours.* Followed hard by the warning: *Cross my words, and your soul will writhe forever in flame.*

Thus was hell invented as a threat for bad behavior. And as a curse of anger. And as a cry of self-loathing. All of which hurt life, and hurt it more when story was joined by an equally unfortunate trend in philosophy.

Philosophy, like story, began as an outcropping of nature. Nature was, in the days before philosophy, constantly crashing against itself as one way of life battled another. Until eventually, there evolved a biological tool for mediating conflict. That tool was self-awareness. Self-awareness came into being when two actions in a sentient brain collided, and instead of the stronger immediately crushing the other, the two were spotted by a perspective-taking neural network. The network examined the colliding actions and realized: *That conflict is in me.* Prompting the further epiphany: *Which means that there's not only a conflict; there's a me.*

With this insight came the brain's experience of a self that was distinct from the flow of consciousness. A self that could step back and decide: *Which of the two conflicting actions is better for my well-being?*

That deciding self felt mighty—yet also inadequate. It was mighty because it floated above the fray like a cloud-borne demigod, empowered to choose while the rest of life crashed mindlessly by. But it was also inadequate because it didn't know *how* to choose: the decision could be evaluated in so many equally plausible ways. Was the better option the one that worked right away, or the one that worked in the long term? And if the long term, then how long? Was it better to sacrifice a little good tomorrow for a big good next year? Or was next year not a far enough horizon? Should the decision be made with ten—or even a hundred—years in view? Out of such dilemmas arose ethics, the brain's systematic effort to answer questions about the best way to live. That effort pushed the brain to take a wider view, stepping outside its immediate emotions to calculate the greater dividends that came from patience, cooperation, and generosity. All of which was positive: connecting us to a possibility beyond our near-term appetites, it grew the space for creative action.

But about five millennia or so ago (see chapter 2), that space was gradually colonized by a less positive trend: the philosophical attempt to seek a master vantage from which all conflicts could be resolved. The master vantage gained the names Truth and Justice, and to derive its global outlook from unassailable first principles, philosophers began fashioning the calculation tool we know now as logic.

Logic replaced philosophy's original fruit of open-minded inquiry with omniscient certainty, restyling the philosopher from an outside perspective into *the only* perspective. And then, sometime around 1000 BCE, in religions such as Zoroastrianism, logic merged with the fable of hell.

This merging replaced the multifarious possibilities of polytheism with the jealous righteousness of One True God. No longer was it possible to consider Zeus from the alternative psychology of Prometheus, or Shiva from the alternative psychology of Vishnu, or Yudi from the alternative psychology of Doumou. Instead, there was only Ahura Mazda, Jehovah, the Almighty.

With the emergence of monotheism, logic's moral commandments were attached to absolute rewards and punishments in the hereafter. Philosophy ascended to meta-physics, then to theology. To trespass the theologians' rational deductions was to risk eternal damnation. It was to be condemned by logic to the underworld imagined by story.

About three decades before Epicurus was born, this logic-story fusion was made manifest by Plato, who in roughly 375 BCE inked it as the final passage of *The Republic*:

> The good things of life are nothing, said Socrates, compared to the prizes and punishments that await the just and the unjust after death. And to show you, I will tell the tale of a hero named Er.
>
> Er died in war, but his body did not rot. And when his body was placed on a funeral pyre, he awoke to reveal that he had seen the afterlife. In that time beyond death, he'd come to a place, between heaven and hell, at which sat a group of judges. The judges sent the just souls to heaven, where they experienced delight and unimaginable beauty; and the judges sent the unjust souls to hell, where they suffered tenfold punishment for every wrong they'd done. Tyrants and other sinners were kept in hell for a thousand years—and then, just when they believed that they would be freed at last from their tortures, they were seized by men of fire, flayed alive, and shredded with thorns.
>
> This story of Er has lived and has not perished. And it will save us if we're obedient to its teachings. So, I advise you, stay true forever to its heavenly way. And walk with justice and virtue always.

In 335 BCE, this "Myth of Er" helped inspire Aristotle's severance of story from thinking (see chapter 2). Three

153

decades later, by the time Leontion walked the Garden, it had become the most popular religious teaching in Athens. And in further days, it was spread by Rome's empire, then by medieval Christianity and Islam, going on to spin off modern, materialist variants like Communism and the Singularity, which promise that if we stick rigorously to logic's dictates, we'll engineer an earthly paradise—or a digital messiah.

Rationally, this has all been for the best. But biologically, it hasn't. That's because our neurons don't input-output the heavenly binary of RIGHT and WRONG; instead, they experiment with neighboring networks to improvise new action scripts (see chapter 6). Our neuroanatomy is thus a fundamentally bad match with the logical architecture of Plato's myth, so even if we uploaded ourselves, like Er, into a realm of immortal being, we wouldn't achieve lasting happiness. We'd be overcome by the sublime beauty; we'd feel a rapture of meaning; then, slowly but inevitably, we'd get bored. We'd wonder: *What other heights can I visit?* And: *What's happening in those misty valleys below?* We'd want, that is, to adventure into the unknown. To test ourselves in uncertain times. And above all, to grow.

As holy light glittered flawlessly, we'd thus feel the urge to escape. Like the gods whose ennui led them to create humanity—and like the subsequent deities who decided to leave their sky mount to grapple with life's hurly-burly—we'd desire more than truth, justice, and perfection forever. We'd hunger to blow up the ideal algorithm and get out.

This is the problem with logical utopias, classical and otherwise. Even if we managed to construct a society of absolute reason, where equality reigned and we could avail ourselves of infinite manna, ambrosia, and panacea, our brain would still want more. Our storythinking synapses are simply not that interested in justice, truth, and other eternally logical fruits. What our narrative brain really craves is new challenges—and new opportunities. The only way to keep our gray matter following the rules (even when the rules are utterly enlightened) is to sedate it with drugs or with fear.

Which is why myths such as Er and the Singularity are—and were, and will always be—sources of human unhappiness. Just as Epicurus perceived in his Garden, logic's fables make our brains feel discontented. They fill us with negative judgments about ourselves and others. They trap us in a state of unhuman regulation. They bless us with tedium unending.

Yet fortunately, we can break the spell of platonic monotony. Because even though Epicurus's ethics didn't completely sync with our psychology, we're now in a position to cultivate a new Garden, one capable of growing human life beyond happiness.

BEYOND HAPPINESS

Our minihistory of story and philosophy reveals that the unhappiness diagnosed by Epicurus is a symptom of the deeper problem caused by Plato's heaven. The deeper problem is that logic limits creative action.

Creative action (as we saw back in chapters 1 and 2) is the root driver of our biology. It's what generated our brain—and what led our brain to generate story and philosophy. Story increased creative action by attuning us to a bigger narrative filled with outside powers. Philosophy increased creative action by lifting us out of our egoistic biases, liberating us to imagine worlds beyond what we feared and wanted.

To recover those life-sustaining possibilities, we need to interrupt the narrowing of story and philosophy that yielded Plato's myth of Er. That narrowing began when we started thinking that our story was more important than others, and it accelerated when we started thinking that philosophy was a tool for finding the one, true plot. So, we must reverse those two processes. We must restore philosophy's original function: to help us exit our lone perspective and to broaden the chances for action. And we must also reclaim story's original function: to help us imagine a broader narrative filled with characters beyond ourselves.

Taken together, these two functions converge on a bigger process: enlarging the stories of outside lives. Or more concretely: expanding other people's creative opportunities. Which we can do by giving those people the intellectual space, emotional confidence, and material support to plan their most original lives.

This is the ultimate *Why* of human existence. Not because it's true, just, or logical. But because it works biologically for our brain. It shifts our attention away from eternal states—such as heaven and happiness—that are counterproductive to our process psychology. And it engages us in the worldly action of growing other storythinking minds.

That action cannot be weakened by even our brain's most powerful fear: death. Death has no grip on a story that goes on beyond us, flowing forward as far as we can imagine. Nor can that action be corrupted by our brain's most potent desire: self-love. To find purpose in nurturing the narratives of others is to channel egoism into its opposite, discovering our immortality in the temporal flourishing of every life we encounter.

Hence the joyous days of many a parent, teacher, mentor, and friend. And hence the way for us to mobilize the ethics that this book's previous chapters have excavated from natural history. Those excavations reveal:

1. That our brain evolved as a storythinker.
2. That storythinking can be further evolved via personal strategies (such as perspective shifting) and social narratives (such as democracy).
3. That such evolutions yield the fun and freedom of physical, emotional, and intellectual growth.

To these three plot points, we can now add:

4. That our personal physical, emotional, and intellectual growth is accelerated by empowering the storythinking of the people around us.

Our better story, in other words, is one where we concentrate on writing books that help readers imagine more books, on building schools that help students invent new ways of learning, and on engineering technologies that help users pioneer fresh breakthroughs.

If we live like this, we'll get up every morning with hope and energy. Not *perfect* hope and energy, because, of course, we're human. But *enough* hope and energy to get the day rolling, and from there to spin through the years, as life's plots absorb us and we find our ultimate reason in using our biography to grow the biographies of others. Aka, narrative generosity, or storygiving.

Such giving is what Epicurus did when he invited Leontion into the Garden. And although Leontion vanished from history's scroll soon after, perhaps she carried on the gift in unrecorded deeds, growing the chances of other lives, helping them tend their own Gardens, unique and branching. Perhaps she became, as the English novelist George Eliot imagined twenty-three centuries later, one of those unremembered souls whose effect "on those around her was incalculably diffusive: for the growing good of the world is partly dependent on unhistoric acts; and that things are not so ill with you and me as they might have been, is half owing to the number who lived faithfully a hidden life, and rest in unvisited tombs."

And perhaps that can be our story, too.

Coda

Conversations with a Storythinker

My *y time is short and this book is long. Can you summarize it for me?*

1. Philosophers have historically tried to reduce all intelligence to symbolic logic, which includes induction, deduction, interpretation, critical thinking, dialectic, math, statistics, data-driven decision making, rational choice theory, homo economicus, systems 1 and 2, divergent thinking, convergent thinking, design thinking, Bayesian inference, IQ, and computer AI.

2. But the human brain runs another form of intelligence, narrative intelligence, that can't be reduced to logic. Narrative intelligence powers counterfactual thinking (or, *what if* thinking), causal thinking (or, speculating *why*), and other mental actions that drive creativity, adaptability, and low-data decision making in volatile and uncertain environments.

3. Narrative intelligence is an engine of empirical science, medicine, engineering, business, technological innovation, and psychological resilience. It's what allows us to thrive

in dynamic domains, which, despite the best efforts of AI logistics and rational civilization to impose eternal order, inevitably result from the asymmetric contests of biological life.

▶ ▷ ▶

A lot of what you call narrative—like causal and counterfactual thinking—sounds to me like logic.
You're using the word "logic" in its colloquial sense, as opposed to its rigorous formal definition.

When we call something "logical" in ordinary conversation, we're typically referring to narrative, not logic. That's because most of us base our views of what is reasonable upon lived experience, history, and other empirical observations that we errantly claim as inductions—and that we use to draw what we mistakenly call deductions. In fact, our "inductions" are exceptional information (i.e., a few vivid events that seem highly significant), and our "deductions" are causal and counterfactual thinking (i.e., hypothesizing *why* something happened and imagining *what might* result).

This reliance on narrative intelligence is why ordinary folk diverge on what they see as "logical." And why philosophers have long criticized nonphilosophers for being sloppy thinkers. But that doesn't mean that nonphilosophers are guilty of mental incompetence. They're simply deploying a different form of acumen, one that recognizes that in our constantly changing biological world, there can be multiple good ways to act.

▶ ▷ ▶

Why are you so certain that narrative intelligence can't be reduced to logic?
There are deductive proofs (like the one in chapter 5). But the empirical giveaway is the human brain, which contains two different neural mechanisms that evolved more than 500 million years ago to perform distinct biological functions: vision and action.

Vision employs the mechanics of symbolic logic, including representation, equation, pattern recognition, meaning, and sense making. Action employs the mechanics of narrative, including experimentation, speculation, process recognition, planning, and use making.

Each of these ancient neural mechanisms takes up significant space in our modern head. This wouldn't be the case if either mechanism could be reduced to the other: evolution would have slowly relegated the unnecessary mechanism to a biological appendix, making our brain more efficient.

What our brain's dual mechanisms thus reveal is that narrative and logic are complementary tools. There's no way to replace storythinking with deduction or interpretation, any more than there's a way to replace a hammer with a saw.

▶ ▷ ▶

Could you define storythinking?
Storythinking is a synonym for narrative cognition, or in other words, thinking in *actions* (as opposed to thinking in equations, meanings, representations, symbols, numbers, and other logical stuff.) So, it's nonsemantic and noncomputational. It's not used for sense making; it's used for

planning, plotting, strategizing, and in other ways creating new behaviors and courses of action.

Storythinking includes causal thinking (i.e., speculating on *why* something happened), scientific hypothesizing (i.e., predicting what *will* happen in response to specific interventions), counterfactual thinking (i.e., imagining what *could* have happened if past events were changed), and outright fiction (i.e., inventing alternate worlds). It proceeds by manipulating the elements of story, of which the big four are: characters, storyworlds, plots, and narrators.

- Characters are causal actors; the causes of their behavior are usually hopes, fears, desires, and other psychological motives.
- Storyworlds are environments with their own distinct laws of action, that is, rules about what can and cannot happen. Such rules can be social, natural, magical, etc.
- Plots are the specific sequences of action generated by characters in a storyworld.
- Narrators are the ultimate cause of the story. They are *why* it is told, and their *why* shapes *how* it is told.

All four elements are anchored in our brain's biology, which evolved to keep us alive by processing other people's psychological motives (characters); by onboarding the rules of new environments (storyworlds); by explaining and predicting emergent threats, opportunities, and other changes in our physical vicinity (plots); and by connecting all of these happenings to our own *why* (narrator).

▶ ▷ ▶

What's the relationship between storythinking and narrative intelligence?
Narrative intelligence is the application of storythinking to solve practical problems and invent practical technologies.

Because storythinking evolved to keep us alive, it tends naturally toward intelligent outcomes. But it's possible for storythinking to detach from sustainable biological uses, becoming inexact and wish fueled. When that happens, it becomes *magical thinking.*

Narrative intelligence is the conscious manifestation of a deeper form of brainpower, motor intelligence, that drives the spontaneous problem solving and innovation of our bodily limbs, making possible the nonconscious improvisation of dancers, athletes, musicians, and other physical performers.

The shorthand for motor intelligence is *moto.* Anytime your body has reacted smartly to an unprecedented situation, you've experienced moto.

▶ ▷ ▶

No offense, but this book makes a lot of very big claims that contradict the mainstream views of most people (philosophers or not) who consider themselves rational. What's the factual basis for its idiosyncratic assertions?
This book's assertions have three bases:

1. *Narrative theory.* Narrative theory dates back to Aristotle, and its modern practitioners have turned up troves of empirical evidence that rebut the popularly held view that literature can be reduced to language (which is to say, that stories can be analyzed via semiotics). A basic example of

this evidence is action verbs, which (as detailed in chapter 5) cannot be processed via symbolic logic, leading to the fundamental inability of computer Natural Language Processors such as GPT-4 to comprehend or reproduce novels, screenplays, etc.

2. *Neuroscience.* Ever since the pioneering dissections of Nobel Laureate Santiago Ramón y Cajal in the late nineteenth century, neuroscientists have uncovered the neuron's anatomical complexity, a complexity fundamentally unlike the elegant simplicity of computational logic gates. From the perspective of storythinking, the most significant feature of the neuron's complexity is the synapse, which (as detailed in chapter 6) distinguishes our brain from computers by providing a nonelectronic architecture that makes possible causal thinking and other forms of narrative cognition.

3. *Scientific experiments.* As recommended by Karl Popper (see chapter 6), the theories outlined in this book have been submitted to tests of falsifiability. In collaboration with partners from U.S. Special Operations to Midwestern public school districts, my lab at Ohio State's Project Narrative has run randomized controlled trials that have shown that narrative training can significantly increase creative problem solving and psychological resiliency.

None of this proves, of course, that the assertions of the preceding pages are true. But some quick self-inspection of your own mental processes—which include planning, speculating on *why* events happen, and imagining *what if*—should be enough to demonstrate that storythinking is as philosophically plausible as Descartes's *Cogito.*

▶ ▷ ▶

The root justification for philosophy isn't just the identification of intelligence but the improvement of intelligence. Traditional philosophy has helped students get better at logic. Can students also get better at storythinking?

Yes. As described in chapters 2 and 4, students can improve their storythinking by consuming and producing narrative art, from ancient epics to sci-fi comics. And as detailed in chapter 7, they can make this training more rigorous via methods that replace critical thinking, interpretation, and the other logic-based techniques used to analyze literature in modern classrooms with techniques derived from the creative mechanisms of biological evolution.

165

▶ ▷ ▶

What's the relationship of narrative intelligence to emotion?

Narrative and emotion are tightly connected in the human brain, because both involve action.

Emotion is the instigator of action. We're more likely to act if we *feel* we should than if we simply *think* we should. That's because feelings such as desire and fear are more potent psychological motivators than beliefs about what's RIGHT or TRUE.

Narrative is the director of action. It tells us *where* to flee when we are scared, and *how* to chase when we are keen. It provides the plans, plots, and strategies for getting what we want—and escaping what we hate.

Which is to say: emotion is human behavior's engine and narrative its steering wheel.

▶ ▷ ▶

What's the relationship of narrative intelligence to emotional intelligence?
Emotional intelligence is less a coherent form of intelligence than a catchall term for a wide variety of theories, some more scientifically valid than others, that collectively resist the effort to reduce all smart behavior to logic. That resistance broadly aligns the proponents of emotional intelligence with the researchers of narrative intelligence.

More specifically, emotional intelligence can include mental activities such as empathy and emotional self-regulation that (as described in chapters 8, 9, and 10) fall under the branch of narrative intelligence known as ethics.

► ▷ ►

By eschewing logic and metaphysics, doesn't storythinking set philosophy back five thousand years, eliminating pretty much every philosopher we study today (and every book and article ever written about them)?
Storythinking doesn't delete logic or metaphysics; it simply restricts them to their own domain, distinct from ethics and real-world action.

► ▷ ►

That's the equivalent of saying that philosophy is useless.
Or that philosophy can expand into a huge new domain: narrative cognition.

► ▷ ►

Don't you think that metaphysics and logic are useful for anything?

They're useful for solving metaphysical and logical problems, just not for solving ethical or biological problems such as personal and social growth.

► ▷ ►

I don't see what's new here. Previous philosophers have already spent a lot of time emphasizing uniqueness (e.g., William Ockham's nominalism) and perspective shifting (e.g., Friedrich Nietzsche's perspectivism).

Previous philosophers have emphasized the uniqueness of individual *objects* and taken the perspective of different *beliefs*. Storythinking emphasizes the uniqueness of individual *actions* and takes the perspective of different *doers*.

That's why Ockham and Nietzsche malfunction logic, while the techniques of storythinking—like prioritizing the exceptional and stoking narrative conflict—*function* creative action, increasing the originality, diversity, and sustainability of human plotting.

► ▷ ►

How would philosophers go about studying narrative cognition?
They'd apply the same rigor to narrative that they've applied to logic.

So, narrative would be rigorously studied as a process, not a product. Causes would be rigorously treated as mechanically unique. The laws of storyworlds would be

167

made rigorously consistent. Narrative conflict would be rigorously methodized to hit the generative sweet spot between sterile peace and destructive strife.

And crucially, narrative would be distinguished from logic without being subordinated to it. Students would be discouraged from judging stories as RIGHT or WRONG, TRUE or FALSE. Instead, they'd be encouraged to value stories for being original, specific, and organically coherent.

▶ ▷ ▶

What makes narrative conflict different from dialectic and other forms of logical disagreement?

Narrative conflict involves a collision of actors, motives, rules of action, etc. So, in contrast to logical disagreement, which is symmetric and stably directed, narrative conflict is asymmetric, volatile, and nonteleological, like the clash that Clausewitz detected in war and Darwin in life. It's generative of new actions, actors, and plots—until it blows apart.

▶ ▷ ▶

Why can't philosophers apply logic to narrative?
Logic un-narratives narrative, creating fables with morals, myths with archetypes, heavens with commandments, stories with symbols, media with representations, and other timeless interpretations that evaporate storythinking's core function: the innovation of action.

▶ ▷ ▶

If we knew everything, wouldn't logic replace storythinking?
Yes, but until we reach that impossible future, we'll want to toggle between logic and storythinking. Logic treats rules as absolute, so it's dependable as long as the rules hold. Storythinking treats rules as useful tools, so it's able to invent new rules when the old ones fail.

Logic generates reliability. Storythinking, creativity. Logic uses the past to predict the future; storythinking breaks from the past to *make* the future.

Logic is intelligent design. Storythinking is biological evolution.

Humans have a long history of valuing intelligent design, from Plato's *Timaeus* to medieval theology to Stanford's d.school. But the main historical driver of better societies and technologies is storythinking's neural refinement of the evolutionary processes that have birthed nature's myriad wonders.

I understand that this is a book for philosophers, and philosophers are only theoretically pragmatic. But still, I was hoping for more specific, practical tips on improving storythinking.
You can get dozens of specific, practical tips in other works I've authored:

- *The Art of Story* (Great Courses)
- *Wonderworks* (Simon and Schuster)
- *Creative Thinking: A Field Guide* (U.S. Army)
- "3 Exercises to Boost Your Team's Creativity" (*Harvard Business Review*)

► ▷ ►

Okay, but if I don't want to read more of your books, what can I do to improve my storythinking?

The key is to develop your brain's natural capacities for *why* and *what if* thinking, allowing you to plot, plan, and strategize more creatively, adaptively, and variously. So, to get started . . .

- Read stories, like candid memoirs and near-future science fiction, that enlarge your sense of possible mental and physical actions. And read stories, like Shakespearean dramas and subplotted novels, that encourage you to inhabit different psychologies simultaneously.
- Seek out the strange, the unusual, the unconventional— *and suspend your judgments.* Instead of evaluating outliers as good or bad, or rationalizing them to fit your existing worldview, actively speculate: *What new life opportunities could they create?*
- Practice imagining, as precisely as possible, the mechanical steps that would follow from a future action. This jumps you into the future without leaping you into magical thinking.

► ▷ ►

Does growth always require conflict?

Yes. Growth is the action of life, which is driven by the asymmetric conflict of evolution by natural selection.

That doesn't mean that conflict is always—or only—a source of growth. It can also cause destruction.

But it does mean that our logic-focused culture—with its emphasis on psychological states such as harmony, tranquility, happiness, and peace—underrates the benefits of conflict, both conflict with others and conflict with ourselves.

Conflict with others is the inevitable result of a relationship with any person different from yourself. And conflict with oneself is the inevitable result of having a brain, because a brain is composed of neurons acting democratically (see chapter 3).

Both kinds of conflict can cause discomfort. Which is why our world abounds with putative remedies, like curated friend groups and mindfulness apps. But there's nothing intrinsically wrong with conflict or its social and mental by-products, like tension and anxiety. If the energy from those struggles is used to power creative problem solving, it can produce flow, earned satisfaction, and growth's other psychological benefits.

171

▶ ▷ ▶

What's the most effective way to channel conflict into growth?
Story.

Story, as every playwright knows, starts with a conflict. Conflict between people, or *within* people, is the engine that drives plots along.

Those plots develop over time. And as they develop, they develop our understanding of the consequences of different actions.

The same story process drives the narrative development of every human life and community, powering growth.

▶ ▷ ▶

Do you believe that stories can be TRUE or FALSE?
No. I only believe that they can be helpful or harmful.

▶ ▷ ▶

Ha! I knew it! You're a relativist!
I'm a biologist, so I believe that stories—like teeth and
eyes and minds—are practical tools. But I don't subscribe
to ethical relativism. For starters, even though I don't
believe that stories can be true, I do believe that they can be
honest. Which is to say: they can accurately express the
memories, feelings, and intentions of the people who
think and share them.

And I also don't believe in using stories to manipulate
others. I believe in using them to grow ourselves.

If you turn propagandist and employ story to incite fear
and love, you'll harm the world and do yourself no lasting
good: the narratives you spin will be fragile, because they
draw only on your narrow personal experience, forsaking
the robust diversity of life.

But if you instead feed your brain stories that grow your
own capacity for curiosity, creativity, and courage, you'll
launch a narrative that will outlive you. And if you give
other people the tools to feed themselves those stories,
you'll launch narratives that will live further still.

▶ ▷ ▶

*I have so many questions, like about whether our natural,
mental emphasis on consciousness (which, because it's mostly*

visual in our brain, is skewed toward the symbolic and the logi-cal) has narrowed philosophy of mind; whether storythinking offers a mechanical explanation for practical intuitions; and whether time operates differently in narrative and logic. Do these questions make sense?
Yes, but if I said any more, I'd be guilty of having a conversation with myself.

▶ ▷ ▶

If stories make you smarter, then why aren't TV binge-watchers running the world?
What makes you smarter isn't mass quantities of one narrative formula. It's stretching your brain to consume stories outside your current operational range. Which is why Disney is dangerous. And why this book doesn't recycle the same story recipe across all its chapters. Instead, it models different species of plot and character, each of which provides different challenges and opportunities for your brain's narrative machinery.

▶ ▷ ▶

If narrative cognition is a mechanistic process, then couldn't we someday build a noncomputer machine that storythinks?
Yes. See my published work on Artificial Intelligence.

▶ ▷ ▶

For someone so influenced by pessimistic, even cynical, thinkers such as Darwin and Machiavelli, your view of ethics and human social relations is remarkably optimistic.

As a child, l learned: the longer we stand in the dark, the better our eyes get at detecting glimmers of light.

▶ ▷ ▶

Don't you worry that your exclusion of timeless truths and moral principles from ethics and creative action could lead storythinking to be abused by corporations and militaries?
Storythinking is part of life, and the law of life is growth through variety. Go against that law, and you can't prosper for long.

So, yes, corporations and militaries can abuse storythinking, like they can abuse any other tool. And by doing so, they can damage lives. But they also seed their own destruction, from which life—and storythinking—can rebound.

▶ ▷ ▶

You mention in chapter 1 that you studied neuroscience—and also narrative theory? I've heard of neuroscience. But what exactly is narrative theory?
Narrative theory is a diverse body of scholarship published today in journals such as *Narrative* and *The Journal of Narrative Theory*. My particular branch is rhetorical narrative theory, which started with Aristotle's *Poetics* (see chapter 2), was revived in the 1950s by the Chicago School (see chapter 4), and has been continued by scholars such as Distinguished University Professor James Phelan at Ohio State's Project Narrative, where I sit now, writing this book.

▶ ▷ ▶

Maybe I could better grasp your perspective if I knew where your story started.
In the 1980s, when I was young, I read J. R. R. Tolkien and came to believe in right actions and wrong. After which, I went to school and came to believe in good grades and bad.

But then I read William Shakespeare, Frederick Douglass, Charles Darwin, and Maya Angelou. And I changed to believe in positive struggle, creative growth, and branching lives.

► ▷ ►

Where do you think our story goes from here?
Hopefully into schools that place as much emphasis on story and creative action as on logic and critical thinking.

► ▷ ►

And after that?
Anywhere.

Notes

Chapter 1: Quotes from *Hamlet* taken from *The First Folio* (London, 1623), lns. 862, 256–57, 1710, 143–44.

Chapter 2: The Sumerian tale quoted from "The Debate between Summer and Winter: Composite Text," available at Oxford University's *The Electronic Text Corpus of Sumerian Literature (ETCSL)*, https://etcsl.orinst.ox.ac.uk, as text number 5.3.3. "I know that I know nothing" is reported in Diogenes Laertius, *Lives of the Eminent Philosophers*, 2.5.32. Aristotle makes the law of non-contradiction the first principle of metaphysics in *Metaphysics* 4.4.

Chapter 3: Aristotle expresses his views on why literature is more plausible and therefore more scientific than history in *Poetics* 1451. Cicero discusses *narratio* in *Ad Herennium* 1.8.11–1.9.16; *De Inventione* 1.19–21; *Topica* 25.97; and *De Oratore* 2.80.326–2.81.330. The advice to Harvard MBAs can be found in Jill Avery, "Brand Storytelling," Harvard Business School Technical Note 519-049, January 2019. (Revised October 2020.)

Chapter 4: The quotes from the "Language Arts" of the Common Core can be found at http://www.corestandards.org/ELA-Literacy/CCRA/R/. A history of the Chicago School is provided in Vincent B. Leitch, "The Chicago School," in *American Literary Criticism from the Thirties to the Eighties* (New York: Columbia University Press, 1988), 60–80. On I. A. Richards's method of "close reading" and its (complex) relation to New Criticism, see Joseph North, "What's 'New Critical' about 'Close Reading'? I. A. Richards and His New Critical Reception," *New Literary History* 44 (2013): 141–57. For the character

NOTES

critics' reading of *Hamlet*, see Samuel Taylor Coleridge's claim that "Hamlet's character is the prevalence of the abstracting and generalizing habit over the practical," from Coleridge's *Lecture on Hamlet (1818)*, printed in *Lectures and Notes on Shakspere and Other English Poets*, ed. T. Ashe (London: George Bell and Sons, 1897), 531. The single use of "abstract" in *Hamlet* can be found in *The First Folio*, line 1565.

Chapter 5: For my scholarship on why AI cannot process or generate original actions, rendering it incapable of writing novels, innovating technology, or doing science, see (for literary audiences) "Why Computers Will Never Read (or Write) Novels: A Logical Proof and a Narrative," *Narrative* 29 (2021): 1–28, and (for computer science audiences) "Why Computer AI Will Never Do What We Imagine It Can," *Narrative* 30 (2022): 1–30. Short portions of the latter are reproduced with permission in the "What Semiotics Misses" section of chapter 4. McCulloch and Domarus's book, *Lekton, being a belated Introduction by Warren S. McCulloch to The Logical Structure of Mind: An inquiry into the philosophical foundation of psychology and psychiatry by Eilhard von Domarus*, was made publicly available on January 1, 1965, and can be located at https://ntrs.nasa.gov/citations/19650017787. McCulloch and Pitts's coauthored article is "A Logical Calculus of the Ideas Imminent in Nervous Activity," *Bulletin of Mathematical Biophysics* 5 (1943): 115–33. Hobbes's claim that "Reason is computation . . . is addition and subtraction," "Per Ratiocinationem autem intelligo computationem . . . Recidit itaque ratiocinatio omnis ad duas operationes animi Additionem & Substractionem," can be found in "Computation or Logic," in *De Corpore, Book 1, Chapter 1, Section 3*. Turing's quote can be found in Alan Turing, "On Computable Numbers, with an Application to the *Entscheidungsproblem*," *Proceedings of the London Mathematical Society, Series 2* 42 (1936–37): 230–65; corrections, 43 (1937): 544–46. Claude Shannon's master's thesis is "A Symbolic Analysis of Relay and Switching Circuits," Massachusetts Institute of Technology, 1940.

Chapter 6: For more on the neuroscience of storythinking, see Angus Fletcher and Mike Benveniste, "A New Approach to Training Creativity: Narrative as an Alternative to Divergent Thinking," *Annals of the New York Academy of Science* 1512 (2022): 29–45. I. J. Good's quote about the two components of a computer is: "a finite set of symbols together with a finite number of rules of transformation for transforming finite strings of symbols into other strings." I. J. Good, "Logic of Man and Machine," *New Scientist*, April 15,

1965, 182. On the "war" between the soups and the sparks, see E. S. Valenstein, *The War of the Soups and the Sparks: The Discovery of Neurotransmitters and the Dispute Over How Nerves Communicate* (New York: Columbia University Press, 2006). For Herschel's rethinking of the scientific method, see *A Preliminary Discourse on the Study of Natural Philosophy* (London: Longman, Green, Taylor, 1830), 6.171. For Whewell's claim that Herschel had switched the scientific method from induction to "guessing," see [William Whewell], "Herschel's Preliminary Discourse," *Quarterly Review* 45 (1831): 401. "A beam of light as an electromagnetic field" is from Albert Einstein (1951), "Autobiographical Notes," in *Albert Einstein-Philosopher Scientist*, 2nd ed., ed. P. A. Schilpp (New York: Tudor Publishing, 1951), 52–53. John Eccles revealed his debt to Karl Popper as "I was urged by Popper to formulate the electrical hypotheses of synaptic excitation and inhibition in models that invited experimental testing and falsification," John C. Eccles, "My Scientific Odyssey," *Annual Review of Physiology* 39 (1977): 6. Dale's remark about Eccles's "newfound enthusiasm" can be found in John C. Eccles, "From Electrical to Chemical Transmission in the Central Nervous System," *Notes and Records of the Royal Society, London* 30 (1976): 219–30. The natural history of neurons and synapses is murky and marked by rival hypotheses, but for a helpful introduction, see Tomás J. Ryan and Seth G. N. Grant, "The Origin and Evolution of Synapses," *Nature Reviews Neuroscience* 10 (2009): 701–12. Carl von Clausewitz remarks, "Der Krieg ist das Gebiet der Ungewißheit; drei Vierteile derjenigen Dinge, worauf das Handeln im Kriege gebaut wird, liegen im Nebel einer mehr oder weniger großen Ungewißheit," "War is the realm of uncertainty; three-quarters of the things on which action in war is built lie in the fog of a greater or lesser degree of uncertainty." *On War*, Book 1, Chapter 3.

Chapter 7: For "always the one . . . constant story," see Joseph Campbell, *The Hero with a Thousand Faces* (New York: Pantheon, 1949), 1. For examples of how to translate these three general approaches into specific training exercises, see Angus Fletcher, "3 Exercises to Boost Your Team's Creativity," *Harvard Business Review*, March 24, 2022; and Angus Fletcher, *Creative Thinking: A Field Guide to Building Your Strategic Core* (Ft. Leavenworth, KS: U.S. Army Command and General Staff College, 2021).

Chapter 8: On Peirce, Dewey wrote: "The course is very mathematical, and by Logic, Mr. Peirce means only an account of the physical sciences, put in mathematical form as far as possible." Quoted in George Dykhuizen, *The*

NOTES

Life and Mind of John Dewey (Carbondale and Edwardsville: Southern Illinois University Press, 1973), 30–31. For Dewey on the relationship between struggle and growth, see the opening of *Democracy and Education* (1916): "As long as [the living thing] endures, it struggles to use surrounding energies in its own behalf. It uses light, air, moisture, and the material of soil. To say that it uses them is to say that it turns them into means of its own conservation. As long as it is growing, the energy it expends in thus turning the environment to account is more than compensated for by the return it gets: it grows." For Dewey on story, see *Schools of To-morrow*, cowritten with Evelyn Dewey (1915): "The story telling and dramatization are very closely connected and (up to the age of about ten) take the place of the usual bookwork. Stories of literary value, suited in subject matter to the age of the pupils, are told or read to them, and they in turn are asked to tell stories they have heard outside of school. After the ninth or tenth year, when the children have learned to read, they read stories from books either to themselves or aloud, and then the whole class discuss them" (35). Hegel discusses *becoming* [das Werden] in *Wissenschaft der Logik*, book 1, section 1, chapter 1, heading c, e.g., "Das reine Seyn und das reine Nichts ist also dasselbe. Was die Wahrheit ist, ist weder das Seyn, noch das Nichts, sondern daß das Seyn in Nichts, und das Nichts in Seyn . . . das Werden." "Pure being and pure nothing are therefore the same thing. What the truth is, is neither being nor nothing, but being into nothing, and nothing into being . . . that is, becoming." Thomas Henry Huxley, *Ethics and Evolution* (London: Macmillan and Co,, 1893), 81. John Dewey, "Evolution and Ethics," *The Monist* 8 (1898): 330, 340.

Chapter 9: Machiavelli's December 10 letter is to Francesco Vettori. His quote on actions is: "che gli uomini nel procedere loro, è tanto più nelle azioni grandi, debbono considerare i tempi, e accommodarsi a quegli. E coloro che, per cattiva elezione o per naturale inclinazione, si discordono dai tempi, vivono, il più delle volte, infelici, ed hanno cattivo esito le azioni loro, al contrario l'hanno quegli che si concordano col tempo," *Discorsi* 3.8. "Here we see the Roman Senate's great prudence" is 1.38. His anecdotes of Horatius Cocles, Cincinnatus, and Manlius Capitolinus are 1.24, 1.25, 1.8. His claim that the diversity of republics gives them better fortune than princedoms is 3.9. Machiavelli's "The work of this narrative" is "aiutato da coloro che mi hanno, ad entrare sotto questo peso, confortato, credo portarlo in modo, che ad un altro resterà breve cammino a condurlo a loco destinato," Preface, book 1. Francis Bacon, "New Atlantis: A Work Unfinished," in *Sylva Sylvarum*

(London, 1627), 1–47; the term "diverse" appears dozens of times, especially on 32–47. "Men are born free and yet are everywhere in chains" is "L'homme est né libre, & partout il est dans les fers," *Du contrat social; ou, Principes du droit politique* (Amsterdam: Marc Michel Rey, 1762), book 1, chapter 1, page 3. Thomas Paine, *Common Sense* (Philadelphia: W. T. Bradford, 1776), 129.

Chapter 10: On Leontion, see Diogenes Laertius, *Lives of the Eminent Philosophers* 10.5, 10.23. For Epicurus on happiness, see Diogenes Laertius, esp. 10.122–54. Plato's myth of Er is *Republic*, Book 10, 614–21. George Eliot, *Middlemarch: A Study of Provincial Life* (London: William Blackwood and Sons, 1871–72), 8 vols., vol 8, Finale.

Index

INDEX

British Empire, 48
business, 10, 18, 45, 68, 72, 96, 116,
    159
Byzantium, ancient, 48, 115

Campbell, Joseph, 100–103, 105,
    108–9, 179
Camus, Albert, 14
Cataline, 38–39
causal thinking, 4, 45, 52, 90, 95,
    105, 134–35, 159, 162, 164, 170
causes and effects, 4, 13, 24, 45,
    54, 74–76, 79, 88, 104–7,
    109, 132
character criticism, 52, 54, 76
Chicago School, 49–50, 174, 177
Cicero, 37–41, 177
Clausewitz, Carl von, 98, 168, 179
close reading, 54, 56, 177
cognitive science, 55, 72
Coleridge, Samuel Taylor, 178
Common Core, 9, 48–50, 53, 56–57,
    59, 62, 79, 177
computation, 9, 66, 69, 71, 79, 118,
    178
computational theories of mind, 71
computers, 6–10, 18, 33, 61–63,
    70–71, 73, 75–76, 78–79, 96–98,
    164, 178; Arithmetic Logic Unit,
    7, 70; CPU, 71, 96
computer vs. neuron, 43
conflict, 13, 22, 82, 104, 109, 118–19,
    122, 136–39, 151–52, 170–71;
    asymmetric, 12, 98, 104, 107, 121,
    160, 168, 170; narrative, 12, 14–15,
    59, 112, 136–37, 167–68
Confucius, 20, 25–26

convergent thinking, 7, 107, 159
Copernican Revolution, 88
Copernicus, Nicolas, 88, 90
counterfactual thinking, 4, 45, 53,
    135, 160, 162, 170
Crane, Ronald Salmon, 121
creative action, 3–4, 10, 25, 46, 78,
    102, 133, 152, 155–56, 167, 174–75
creative thinking, 92, 94–97, 103,
    105–6, 125, 134, 145, 169, 179
creativity, 6–7, 16, 42, 44–45,
    78–79, 105, 108–9, 156, 159, 169,
    172; and growth, 124;
    neuroscience of. See narrative,
    neuroscience of; and science, 89
creativity training, 178
critical thinking, 6, 10, 53, 56, 62,
    79, 95, 107, 159, 165, 175
Curie, Marie, 15–16

Darwin, Charles, 15, 89–90, 95, 97,
    109, 113–14, 118–20, 168, 173, 175
Darwinian evolution, 4, 103, 119, 121
Darwinism, social, 120
data, 8, 38, 41, 43, 53, 62, 72–73, 85,
    89, 95, 98
da Vinci, Leonardo, 6
Delacroix, Charles, 121
Descartes, René, 6, 26, 164
design thinking, 7, 10, 62–63,
    72–73, 78, 96–97, 159, 169
Dewey, John, 112–13, 116–22, 134,
    179–80
Disney, 173
divergent thinking, 159, 178
Domarus, Eilhard von, 63–65, 68,
    73, 76, 98, 178

INDEX